Shakespeare and the Human Mystery

J. Philip Newell

Paulist Press
New York/Mahwah, N.J.

First published in Great Britain in 2003
Azure
1 Marylebone Road
NW1 4DU

Published in the United States in 2003
Paulist Press
997 Macarthur Boulevard
Mahwah, N.J. 07430

Quotations from the plays of William Shakespeare
are taken from
The New Penguin Shakespeare
(Harmondsworth: Penguin)

A CIP record for this book is available from
the Library of Congress

ISBN: 0-8091-4249-X

Typeset by FiSH Books, London
Printed in Great Britain

Contents

To the bard of St Giles

Gilleasbuig Macmillan

Preface

Ben Jonson, the seventeenth-century English dramatist, claimed that his contemporary William Shakespeare was a man born not for his age alone but for all time. Four hundred years later and Jonson's prophetic words are still ringing true. Certainly for me, from as early as I can remember, the name of Shakespeare has been part of my general consciousness. There are primary school memories of *Romeo and Juliet* and a half-awareness that somehow it related to what I was feeling about the girl next to me in class, although I never managed to express it. Or there are adolescent memories of studying *Julius Caesar* and knowing within something of the pain of human betrayal. Year after year in my life, like century after century for countless others, I have chosen to place myself before his characters to watch in them something that also is in me. The experience is sometimes laughter, sometimes tears, sometimes shame. Always it is the experience of looking into a mystery that I am part of.

The writing of this book has been a long project. I have worked on it over a number of years, usually in the early mornings when I watch for the coming dawn and hope for a bit of clarity. It has taken me to different places, both within myself and beyond. Early on I explored the main themes at Plaza Resolana, a study centre in New Mexico, during the 'Shakespeare in Santa Fe' festival. Slightly later was a series of talks at St Giles Cathedral during the Edinburgh International Festival. The latter was a good setting in which to try out the material because week after week St Giles is a place of poetic utterance, thanks to the one to whom I have dedicated this book.

There are a number of people to thank. Alison Barr, my delightful editor, has encouraged the project along its way. And Ali, my merry wife, has been a constant believer, even though she experienced existential doubt when I left the 'Lover and Friend' chapter to move on to the 'Judge and Warrior'. Also there is dear Larry Joplin, a fine embodiment of the friend archetype. When I call him 'Sir John' it is only the best side of Falstaff that I have in mind, usually.

And I am most grateful to my former professor of English literature, Douglas Duncan, for his willingness to comment critically on the manuscript. Although in the past he has rejected my description of him as a 'grotesque exaggeration', I still think he is the best teacher I have known, as well as being a good friend. I suspect though that he will never fully be persuaded that I have not steered Shakespeare into being a supporter of my own vision of humanity. That is a danger in interpreting any great text. I am happy to take the risk. If I have got it terribly wrong I only hope that he and Shakespeare will forgive me.

J. Philip Newell
Edinburgh

Abbreviations

All's Well	*All's Well That Ends Well*
Antony	*Antony and Cleopatra*
As You	*As You Like It*
Comedy	*The Comedy of Errors*
Coriolanus	*Coriolanus*
Cymbeline	*Cymbeline*
Gentlemen	*The Two Gentlemen of Verona*
Hamlet	*Hamlet*
1 Henry IV	*Henry IV: Part One*
2 Henry IV	*Henry IV: Part Two*
Henry V	*Henry V*
1 Henry VI	*Henry VI: Part One*
2 Henry VI	*Henry VI: Part Two*
3 Henry VI	*Henry VI: Part Three*
Henry VIII	*Henry VIII*
John	*King John*
Julius	*Julius Caesar*
Kinsmen	*The Two Noble Kinsmen*
Lear	*King Lear*
Love's Labour	*Love's Labour's Lost*
Macbeth	*Macbeth*
Measure	*Measure for Measure*
Merchant	*The Merchant of Venice*
Merry	*The Merry Wives of Windsor*
Midsummer	*A Midsummer Night's Dream*
Much Ado	*Much Ado About Nothing*
Othello	*Othello*
Pericles	*Pericles*
Richard II	*Richard II*
Richard III	*Richard III*
Romeo	*Romeo and Juliet*

Taming	*The Taming of the Shrew*
Tempest	*The Tempest*
Timon	*Timon of Athens*
Titus	*Titus Andronicus*
Troilus	*Troilus and Cressida*
Twelfth	*Twelfth Night*
Winter	*The Winter's Tale*

Introduction

My focus in this book is the human soul and what it means to be truly alive. I shall be drawing on literary treasure, in particular the treasury of Shakespeare's writings, but this is not primarily a literary study. It is a way of pondering the mystery of our human nature, allowing Shakespeare's characters to be expressions of what is deepest in us. Generation after generation, and even century after century, we return to the texts of Shakespeare. His *dramatis personae* express the life and the shadows that are within us.

What cannot be said about each one of us is always greater than anything that can be said. While we may describe ourselves in terms of gender or religion or nationality, none of these categories, however dear to us, contains the essence of our being. The heart of who we are cannot be captured by any boundary of definition. Again and again Shakespeare conveys this sense of mystery, the undefinableness, the uncontainableness of who we are. In *1 King Henry VI* when the French Countess Auvergne traps the English Lord Talbot in her house she claims that she has him, to which Talbot replies,

> No . . .
> You are deceived. My substance is not here;
> For what you see is but the smallest part
> And least proportion of humanity.
> I tell you, madam, were the whole frame here,
> It is of such a spacious lofty pitch
> Your roof were not sufficient to contain't.
>
> (*1 Henry VI* II 3 49-55)

We tend to see ourselves and one another in terms of what can be defined or measured, our race or religion, our political persuasion or sexual identity. Instead I believe we more often need to see ourselves and one another in terms of what cannot be defined, our essence, and to see that the undefinable mystery that is within us is the

1

common ground that we share with one another and with the whole of humanity and with all creation. We share an origin or beginning that is deeper than any of life's divisions or distinctions. And yet we know so little of what is deepest in us.

As Isabella says in *Measure for Measure*, we are 'most ignorant' of what we are 'most assured', our 'glassy essence' (*Measure* II 2 121–2). We know least about what is most enduring, the diamond core of our being. In *King Richard III* when the Duke of Clarence has been imprisoned and is about to be killed, he has a dream in which he sees sunken treasure-ships with thousands of skeletons at the bottom of the sea. Their bodies have been 'gnawed upon' and eaten by fish, but within the skeletons Clarence sees what he calls 'wedges of gold . . . heaps of pearls, inestimable stones, unvalued jewels' (*Richard III* I 4 26–7). It is a picture of our 'glassy essence', the priceless depths of our being. It is something that no power, not even the power of death, can undo.

As a way of exploring the essence of the human mystery and what it means to truly live from these depths, I will be referring to what can be called archetypes of the soul. The word 'archetype' simply means the first type, or the original pattern. It is a way of pointing to what is first in us, to what is most original in the soul.

In modern psychoanalytical thought Carl Jung speaks about the collective unconscious within us as being composed of countless archetypes. These issue up from the common ground of the human soul. Wholeness, he says, is achieved through an integrating of the archetypes from the realm of the unconscious into the conscious, of consciously becoming reconnected to what is deepest in us and in all people. He calls this process individuation, which he understands as the reintegration of our true self.

Long before Jung, however, the first-century Jewish philosopher Philo uses the term archetypes. He uses it in relation to the *Imago Dei*, the Judaeo-Christian and Islamic belief that humanity is made in the image of God (Genesis 1.27). For Philo the archetypes refer to the essential characteristics of the image of God in us. They are the primary expressions of the original depths of our being. Although the sacred image has been covered over and distorted by wrong and by ignorance, it is still at the core of our being.

My thesis is that instead of living from the foundations of our being, from what can be called the 'Imago', we tend to live from the distortion of our depths, or from what can be called the 'Iago' within us. I am not arguing that Shakespeare had this in mind when he named his character Iago, although he might have. The twisted anti-hero in *Othello* is a distorted or fragmented version of the human mystery. Iago's self-description in the opening scene of *Othello* is 'I am not what I am' (*Othello* I 1 66). He represents the falseness of which we are capable, the perversions into which we sink. This is not to say that the sacred depths of our being have been lost. Rather, they have become twisted, and at times so covered over in our lives and relationships as to appear to have been erased. But deeper than any falseness in us is the true self, the *Imago*, waiting to be healed and recovered.

So there are the archetypes of the soul, which are the expressions of what is deepest in us, and there are the shadows of the archetypes, which are the distortions of what is deepest in us. As one of the French lords says in *All's Well That Ends Well*, 'The web of our life is of a mingled yarn, good and ill together' (*All's Well* IV 3 70–1). Each archetype has a true expression as well as a false expression. The reality is that they are intermingled in our souls. Wholeness is to be found in being reconnected to what is first, but the journey towards wholeness involves a confronting of the shadow and a turning from the false self.

As the Friar in *Romeo and Juliet* picks flowers and herbs from the ground for medicinal use, he says, 'mickle is the powerful grace' that lies in nature (*Romeo* II 3 11–12). In each plant there lives some special goodness. If misused or misapplied, however, the goodness becomes poisonous. It destroys instead of healing. Similarly within us, he says, there are 'powerful graces' for goodness and well-being, but these very graces if twisted become poisonous in our souls. We become destructive instead of creative, selfish instead of self-giving.

In *Troilus and Cressida* Troilus says, 'sometimes we are devils to ourselves' (*Troilus* IV 4 94). Sometimes we allow what has been planted most deeply within us to become distorted or blighted, and the most essential energies of our souls become warped or misdirected. The streams of our inner being begin to flow against life instead of for life. Rather than trusting what is at the heart of our being we become fearful and suspicious. We begin to assume that the shadow is the true face of the soul rather than a clouding or distorting of our original countenance.

What are the true depths or archetypes of the human mystery? They of course cannot be reduced to number. Neither can their content be limited by definition. As many images as there are in dream-life so are there archetypes of the soul. And as impossible as it is to capture the imagery of a dream with fixed explanation so is it impossible to place boundaries of definition on the depths of our inner being. The archetypes shift and merge into one another like reflections of light off flowing waters. The moment we try to hold them still we lose a true sense of the great inner current of the human soul. It is possible to discern patterns in the flow of the soul's life, but any attempt to focus on an archetype is at best like a photographic frame of one portion of a mighty river in motion. The actual content will always surpass the particular image. And yet there is value in noting the clusters of characteristics that gather around particular expressions of the soul.

In the plays of Shakespeare I have identified five such clusters. I explore them in pairs or couplets of archetypes. There is the king and the queen, that dimension of the soul that holds together the inner kingdom of our being, and without which there is chaos and disorder in our lives. There is the lover and the friend, that part of our being which we know only in relationship or in the longings for relationship that stir within us. There is the warrior and the judge who reflect our passion for what is just and right, but whose frightening shadows can assume the form of domination and injustice. There is the seer and the mage in our depths, gifted with inner sight and intuition and the power to glimpse the future and to transform the present. And there is the fool and the contemplative in the soul, alert to the impermanence of all things and to the new beginnings that can be found in letting go.

To be true to these depths is to be truly alive. As Polonius advises his son Laertes in *Hamlet*, 'above all to thine own self be true'. If we are true to our own depths, he says,

> . . . it must follow, as the night the day,
> Thou canst not then be false to any man.

(Hamlet I 3 78–81)

There is an inseparable relationship between our own soul and the soul of all life. To be true to our own depths is to find the pathway towards being true to what is deepest in one another, just as being true to what is deepest in one another is to find the pathway towards being true to our own depths.

In the Appendix are 'Journalling Exercises' which I have used with groups to explore the main archetypes of this study. The method employed is what Carl Jung calls the 'active imagination', in which unconscious material within us is allowed to move into consciousness through a deliberate and uninhibited use of fantasy. Innumerable texts from Shakespeare could be used as the basis for such imaginative interior dialogue. I have simply included five as examples of what can be done. The intention is to enable a healing flow between our unconscious depths and our conscious mind as a way of moving towards a recovery of our original archetypal depths.

I

The King and the Queen

'I shall hereafter... be more myself.'
(*1 Henry IV* III 2 92–3)

The True King and Queen

The treasure-trove of the soul consists of countless archetypes. No single archetype, and not even all of them together, can sum up the mystery of our being. They do, however, point to aspects of who we are. Usually the more ancient and even primordial the archetype the deeper it is pointing. We may not feel like kings and queens today, and most of us do not live in societies in which royalty features dominantly, but the archetype of the king and queen is a way of speaking about that dimension within us that gives cohesion to our inner being. It is that part of the soul that holds together the kingdom of our life. Philosophically we may refer to it as the will, or psychologically as the conscious determining centre of our psyche. It is that part of us that exercises a type of ultimate authority over the other aspects of who we are.

Much of the time the inner realm of our lives may not be held together very well. Our thoughts and emotions, our deep physical and sexual energies, fly in all sorts of directions, often at cross purposes with our intentions and commitments. Sometimes there is a total collapse of integration in our inner being as if the king and queen were not there or as if they had been ousted from their place of power or been forgotten.

We are like the princes in *Cymbeline* who, kidnapped as young boys, grow up not knowing who they are. There continues to be much in them that is royal, 'their thoughts do hit the roofs of palaces', as their adoptive father says of them (*Cymbeline* III 3 83–4), but they live primitively in a cave, stooped over with bowed heads. It is a picture of royalty forgotten or suppressed. It speaks of the gap in us between the conscious self and the true depths of the self. As Prospero says to Miranda in *The Tempest*, thou 'art ignorant of what thou art' (*Tempest* I 2 18). Miranda does not know that she is the heir of Milan. Growing up in exile on a remote island she remembers only as in a dream her childhood in the royal court. She is distant from her place of origin and deepest identity. Spiritually she represents the way in which we live in a type of forgetfulness of what is first in us. At times we live so far from the original sovereignty of our souls that we remember our royalty of being only faintly as in a dream. It is to these depths that we need to be re-awakened if we are to be alive to who we truly are.

To say that there is a royal archetype within the soul is not, of course, to say that we can contain it by definition or understanding. Rather we are naming a part of us which is beyond subjection. It is to be regarded as mystery and not labelled in such a way that we pretend to know exactly what it is, and therefore to have a type of power over it. As Prince Hamlet says to Rosencrantz and Guildenstern, friends of the Danish court who claim to know him and thus to be able to manipulate him, 'how unworthy a thing you would make of me! You would play upon me [like an instrument]. You would seem to know my stops. You would pluck out the heart of my mystery. You would sound me from my lowest note to the top of my compass. . . . 'Sblood, do you think I am easier to be played on than a pipe? Call me what instrument you will, though you can fret me, yet you cannot play upon me' (*Hamlet* III 2 371–9). Although the king/queen in us can be disturbed or unsettled, although it can be distorted and turned into shadow or a falseness of expression, the true royalty of our being will not be controlled by another. It is by definition sovereign. It can never ultimately be under the power of another, even though again and again in our lives we act like slaves, whether outwardly to systems and fashions or inwardly to fears and fantasies.

So what is the true king/queen archetype? In some ways, of course, it is easier to point to what it is not, to describe the shadow side, to say what has gone wrong in our lives and in the inner realm of our souls. The false king/queen is not only easier to describe, it also tends to be more noticeably colourful than the true sovereign. Like Satan in Milton's *Paradise Lost*, false royalty usually upstages good royalty. So it is with Shakespeare's characters. In part this is because the way to the true king/queen archetype is through the false. The journey of reconnection to the truth of our being involves a looking at the shadow and a naming of it, a confronting of the falseness and distortions in us in order to discover and reclaim what is deeper and richer still, the true royalty of our depths.

We know that we have failed, and that at times in our lives the regal part of who we are has been lost sight of or been disempowered. We know about our 'sick soul', as Queen Gertrude calls it in *Hamlet* (*Hamlet* IV 5 17). And we know that when the king or queen in us is not well, or has become twisted and diseased in its aspirations, the whole of the inner kingdom begins to be disturbed, or, as one of the king's soldiers says in the Danish court where terrible wrong has been done by King Claudius, 'something is rotten in the state of Denmark' (*Hamlet* I 5 25). When the king/queen archetype in us is sick the whole kingdom of our life suffers. We become destabilized from the heart of our being outwards. Our energies and desires, our creativities and relationships become misdirected and chaotic.

But deeper than the shadow is the true archetype. As in Shakespeare, amidst the many false expressions of royalty there is the good king/queen. There is Henry V, the true king par excellence, who journeys through misdirected times in his life towards a maturity of sovereignty. It was, says the Archbishop in *King Henry V*, as if 'an angel came and whipped th'offending Adam out of him' (*Henry V* I 1 28–9). His misspent energies of youth are channelled into a true royalty of personhood. He turns from a life in which the marks of his sovereignty had either been lost sight of or been exercised only limitedly. He repents, returning to a sovereign nature that serves the well-being of the entire realm. As his father says of him, pointing to some of the major characteristics of true kingship, 'he is gracious .... He hath a tear for pity, and a hand open as day for melting charity' and yet if he senses wrong 'he is flint, as humorous as winter' and he acts decisively, without hesitation, 'as sudden as flaws congealed in the spring of day' (*2 Henry IV* IV 4 30–5). Henry represents a sovereignty that is compassionate but which in the face of wrong or chaos moves swiftly to re-establish order and well-being. He embodies that aspect of the soul which is capable of taking hold of the varied energies of our being. If left undirected they become confused and destructive. If channelled they can be steered towards creativity and life.

Sovereignty Betrayed

But let us first explore the shadow, the false king and queen who either do not know themselves or who betray their own sovereignty. There is King John who is so insecure in his kingship that he seeks to be crowned again, like a second baptism (*John* IV 2 1). He represents that side of us that can be so unsure of our inner identity that we desperately seek outward assurances to shore up our confidence. We begin to live in relation to the secondary authority of external opinion and whether or not we are liked and approved of, rather than living in relation to the primary authority of who we are and what our soul knows we should be doing.

Or there is Henry VI who neglects his kingly duty in favour of a type of religious piety, so much so that his wife says of him,

> I would the College of the Cardinals
> Would choose him Pope, and carry him to Rome.
>
> (*2 Henry VI* I 3 59–60)

One suspects that he has failed not only as king but as lover. He represents a denial of his true depths under the guise of religious devotion, a misuse of religiosity to cover over his lack of attention to the struggles and delights of kingship and relationship. It is an expression of the way in which we can abdicate responsibility under the banner of respectability. We ignore the soul's sovereignty and passion, and end up living tragically removed from the vibrancy of our true depths.

One of the marks of insecurity of soul is the desire to be surrounded by flatterers rather than by speakers of the truth. As the insecure Julius Caesar says,

> Let me have men about me that are fat,
> Sleek-headed men, and such as sleep a-nights.
>
> (*Julius* I 2 191–2)

Men who think too much, he says, are 'dangerous'. When our soul is uncertain we look to half-truths or to pretence for comfort. We avoid looking too closely at what we have done and become.

The weak King Richard II seeks adulation and refuses criticism. Old John of Gaunt, on his deathbed, speaks truth to the king and says, 'A thousand flatterers sit within thy crown' (*Richard II* II 1 100). Richard is no longer sovereign but 'Landlord of England'. So desperate is the king for praise that he has sacrificed true decisiveness in his leadership to curry favour among the nobility. His kingdom lacks direction and purpose. Frenetically he lets out the land and the resources of the realm in all sorts of directions instead of giving it a powerful cohesion and driving force. As the wise old counsellor of Tyre says to King Pericles, 'they do abuse the king that flatter him' (*Pericles* I 2 38). Flattery feeds the shadow side. When we seek it in our lives, our self-understanding and inner resolve are weakened. Our freedom of soul is undermined.

'He who flatters you,' says the counsellor, 'makes war upon your life' (*Pericles* I 2 45).

Just as flattery misleads from the outside so the king and queen who do not know themselves can be misled from within by a false reading of their own conscience. Henry VIII calls it 'the wild sea' of the conscience (*Henry VIII* II 4 200), in which we hear a confusing variety of voices within ourselves and are easily persuaded to follow the path of least outward resistance. We are carried by the strength of the current at its surface instead of following the deeper course of the soul. In *Henry VI* the king knows from his conscience that the accusations against his faithful friend, the Duke of Gloucester, are false but does nothing to prevent the latter's arrest. As Gloucester is being led away, Henry pathetically says that he can do nothing to help, 'so mighty are his vowed enemies' (*2 Henry VI* III 1 220). And yet if the king cannot help who can? If the sovereign depth of who we are is not firm and decisive, then a price is paid in terms of disorder and falseness in the wider realm of our lives and relationships.

In the case of Henry VI sovereignty is more and more abnegated as he consents to the inflated aspirations of the false lords of the kingdom. As one of them says, 'what we do establish he confirms' (*2 Henry VI* III 1 317). Henry becomes a puppet king. He is a picture of the way in which the authority that is within us can fall under the sway of misdirected and destructive inner forces. We become guided by energies that are life-destroying rather than life-giving and by ways of thinking that fragment rather than serve the unity of our life.

Henry's pattern is to resign instead of reign, the fine line between abandoning power and delegating power. During battle he chooses to leave the direction of conflict entirely to others. So distant has he become from the strength of kingship within himself that even one of his supporters says to him,

> I would your highness would depart the field;
> The queen hath best success when you are absent.
>
> (*3 Henry VI* II 2 73–4)

He sits on a little hill near the battlefield and says, 'To whom God will, there be the victory' (*3 Henry VI* II 5 15).

Again Henry manifests a type of religious self-deception in his neglect of sovereignty. But it is not only religion that we use to obscure a strength of will in our depths. Sometimes we appeal to fate. At other times we argue from logic and the overwhelming odds against us in the particular battles of our lives and world. At times what is most terrifying for us is not our weakness but our strength. When we glimpse something of the might that is in us we also realize that we have to act. We discover that there are fewer places to hide from confronting wrong. We realize that there is a power in our depths that can marshal the energies of our being into a unity of strength. But there is also a cost.

Henry flees from the demands of battle and disguises his true identity. A passing shepherd asks him who he is, to which the king replies, 'More than I seem, and less than I was born to' (*3 Henry VI* III 1 56). In a sense we are all more than we seem. The infinite depths of the human soul, like the boundlessness of the physical universe beyond us, can never be given complete expression. Always there will be more to be said. Forever the depths of the unconscious are like inexhaustible treasure from which we may draw new riches. But when we decide not to live from our depths or to cover over the sovereignty that is within us, Henry's words apply. 'Less than I was born to', he says. They speak of a diminished state of being when we turn from the treasure-house that is within us and shut its gates.

Henry chooses literally to resign his powers, 'although my head still wear the crown,' he says (*3 Henry VI* IV 6 23). To two of the English lords he pronounces,

> I make you both Protectors of this land,
> While I myself will lead a private life
> And in devotion spend my latter days
>
> (*3 Henry VI* IV 6 41–3)

Henry has deceived himself into believing that he can claim the outward status of sovereignty while doing nothing to exercise its reality. He is false to himself and thus to his whole kingdom. He pretends that somehow he can lead a purely 'private' life without collective implications. It is the falseness of thinking that we can enjoy the richness of what is within us without living in relation to that treasure. It is the delusion of claiming to have a sovereign depth while ignoring the implications of what that will mean in our lives and relationships.

Richard II is another king who turns against the royalty of his own person. In his case, it is primarily an inability to withstand the pressure of the external forces ranged against him. He concedes, saying, 'I find myself a traitor with the rest'. He allows the doubt and opposition that are in others to overrule his own sense of self, to the extent that he no longer knows who he is,

> ...Alack the heavy day,
> That I have worn so many winters out
> And know not now what name to call myself!
>
> (*Richard II* IV 1 247–58)

When we betray our own depths we are prone to inner confusions. We become vulnerable to the manipulation of others, sometimes to the point of entirely losing a sense of self.

Richard asks for a mirror to look into,

> That it may show me what a face I have
> Since it is bankrupt of... majesty.

He has been untrue to his own depths, yet still he sees what he calls 'a brittle glory' shining in his reflection. So brittle is the glory, however, that when he dashes the mirror to the ground he knows that like the shattered glass his own inner glory has been 'cracked in an hundred shivers' (*Richard II* IV 1 265–88). It seems broken beyond repair.

Such fragmentation in the soul of the sovereign breeds insecurity throughout the whole realm. In *King John* one of the lords says to the self-doubting king that the people of the nation are filled with anxiety, 'not knowing what they fear, but full of fear' (*John* IV 2 146). Insecurity has its repercussions. Like water that is disturbed at the centre of a pond, so uncertainty at the heart of our being ripples out into every aspect of our lives. This is not to say that a contagion of anxiety throughout a kingdom is based always on an awareness of the instability at its centre. As the king's courtier suggests, we can be afraid without knowing why. Insecurity and self-doubt communicate themselves at many levels in our lives and relationships. A weak sovereignty of soul sends out signals, whether inwardly to other dimensions of our being or outwardly in the various relationships of our lives.

The wound of diffidence in the sovereign exposes the kingdom to dangers from without as well as from within. In *King John* one of the noblemen says,

> This England never did, nor never shall
> Lie at the proud foot of a conqueror
> But when it first did help to wound itself.
>
> (*John* V 7 112–14)

The patterns that apply to the stability of an outward kingdom pertain also to the realm of the soul. We are secure in our whole person only as we are well at our centre. We are strong in our relations with others as we are true to the sovereignty of our own depths.

Sovereignty Lost

In *King Lear* we find a tragic expression of inner doubt and confusion. Lear is a monarch who does not know himself and who proceeds out of his self-ignorance to abdicate the most essential responsibilities of sovereignty. His insecurity of soul leads him desperately to seek the outward approval and praise of his daughters. As Regan and Gonerill say of him, 'he hath ever but slenderly known himself' (*Lear* I 1 292–3). So out of touch is he with his true nature that, like Henry VI, he thinks he can retain the dignity and benefits of royalty without any corresponding action. To his sons-in-law as he divides up the kingdom, he says, 'we still retain the name and all th'addition to a king' (*Lear* I 1 135–6). He denies the reality of kingly relationship, but clings to its title.

As he increasingly turns from the truth of his sovereignty Lear loses nearly every remaining vestige of outward respect in his life. Even his daughters' servants begin to treat him with irreverence, no longer paying heed to his utterances. Lear's initial reaction is to think that something has happened to the world. He says, 'Ho, I think the world's asleep' (*Lear* I 4 47). But in the first instance it is not the world that has fallen asleep. It is Lear who has lost consciousness of his own depths. It is he who has fallen asleep to the sovereignty of his being and to what it means to be king. The world around him simply follows his lead. When we cease to respect our own person we find others treating us likewise. When we forget our own identity it is unlikely that others will remember it for us, although there can be important people in our lives, like Lear's faithful daughter Cordelia and his true friend Kent, who carry a type of memory for us of who we are even when we ourselves have forgotten.

The outward collapse of Lear's world is painful. It leads him further and further into uncertainties of soul. 'I will forget my nature', he says (*Lear* I 5 31). Casting around aimlessly for a knowledge of himself, he asks, 'Doth any here know me?' Then even more desperately, 'Who is it that can tell me who I am?' It is the Fool who replies, 'Lear's shadow' (*Lear* I 4 222–7). Lear is the image of a man living outside of himself. He has become a shadow of his true being, living at a tragic distance from the strength and sovereignty that are within him.

As more and more he experiences his daughters' rejection, Lear says, 'O Fool, I shall go mad!' (*Lear* II 4 281). And he does go mad, the way terrible pain and confusion in our lives can push us, to varying degrees, into unreality and psychosis. The loss of relationship between the conscious self and the unconscious depths of our being is one of the major marks of madness. The frightening dimensions of the unknown take over and our world becomes haunted by demons of the unconscious. It is an extreme form of the unawareness that afflicts us all in different ways, when our shadow side obscures from our conscious self a clear perception of what is true.

Lear loses not only an awareness of his own depths but a sense of the natural order of life. The sexual principle that runs through the whole of creation, renewing its plant forms and regenerating the animal world, now becomes in his eyes a perversion. Instead of seeing it as a dimension of himself, as the basis of his own birth and fatherhood, he fears it:

> The wren goes to 't, and the small gilded fly
> Does lecher in my sight.

> (*Lear* IV 6 110–11)

He sees sexual energy everywhere, which in a sense it is, but he loses a perspective of its naturalness. He has forgotten his own nature and feels threatened by the intercourse of creatures and the natural interflowing of all things.

The extreme responses to sexual energy that we find in our culture, whether those be the exaggerated fears and suspicions of sexual desire at one end of the spectrum or the fixations and insatiable appetite for the sexual at the other, are in fact both expressions of Lear's type of madness. They are the result of not integrating the conscious self with the unconscious. Either to blindly follow the unconscious sexual impulses that course through us or, on the other hand, to try to deny that they are present in us, and to live primarily in fear of them, is a type of madness. It is an imbalance between the conscious and the unconscious that cripples life and destroys relationships.

In the midst of his madness Lear at times expresses an acute alertness to what is happening in his soul and to his need for help. 'Let me have surgeons; I am cut to the brains', he says (*Lear* IV 6 193–4). This feature of madness, so often present in cases of mental disturbance, reflects a type of consciousness of the hell into which he has descended,

> . . . I am bound
> Upon a wheel of fire, that mine own tears
> Do scald like molten lead.
>
> (*Lear* IV 7 46–8)

Yet it is not an awareness that frees him from delusion. By this stage he is living almost entirely out of his shadow side, descending further and further into a spiral of unreality. And the wound of deep inner confusion in the king infects not only his own relationships but the relationships of the entire realm. There is discord and growing conflict throughout the land, the way confusion and madness are rarely self-contained in our lives. They trigger off other expressions of instability and lunacy within us and in those around us.

Lear has forgotten his true self. His insanity leads him also to forget his faithful daughter, Cordelia. He is blind to the goodness and the faithfulness of her nature. The confusions of his own soul are projected onto those around him. At one point, having failed to recognize her, he thinks that she too is intent on harming him,

> If you have poison for me, I will drink it.
> I know you do not love me. . . .
>
> (*Lear* IV 7 71–2)

These words express the heart of his sickness. 'I know you do not love me', he says. The thing that in fact is most certain in his life and on which his well-being most depends, Cordelia's faithfulness to him, is the very thing that he doubts. It is the insanity that we suffer in our souls when we shut down to the affection and love that others have for us, or when in our inner confusions we no longer know on whom we may lean.

When Cordelia seeks a blessing from him as her father and king, he is paralysed by his madness and unable to respond. So removed is he from the dignity of his fatherhood and the depth of his own sovereignty that he cannot hold out his hand in benediction over her. It is a feature of no longer knowing the self. We doubt that we can bring blessing to another. Especially when we are broken we think our presence is incapable of bestowing such a gift, although in fact usually the opposite is true. It is often the knowledge of our own woundedness that enables us to bring help to others. It is the phenomenon of the wounded healer. Knowing ourselves to be broken brings a greater depth of reality to the relationships in which others seek wholeness from us.

The deepest note of tragedy for Lear comes when, over the

murdered body of Cordelia, he utters a sorrow that expresses the cost of having not known himself,

> ...no life
> ...no breath at all? Thou'lt come no more;
> Never, never, never, never, never.
>
> (*Lear* V 3 303–6)

There is an irreversibility to some of the wrongs we do when we betray our depths and bring suffering on others. Some of the pain cannot be undone.

Lear loses contact with the kingship of his being, with disastrous consequences, but never does he entirely lose contact with his own humanity. In his faithless daughters, however, we see a grotesque perversion of human nature. They become monsters in their souls. Albany, the husband of Gonerill, says to her,

> That nature which contemns its origin
> Cannot be bordered certain in itself.
> She that herself will sliver and disbranch
> From her material sap perforce must wither
> And come to deadly use.
>
> (*Lear* IV 2 32–6)

When we are faithless to our origins as daughters and sons or as brothers and sisters, we become unnatural in the most important relationships of our lives. When we deny the deep bonds that are part of our genesis we become like branches severed from their roots. Gonerill is a 'changed and self-covered thing' (*Lear* IV 2 62), says Albany. Sin has 'be-monstered' her. It has infected the face of her inner being. So perverted has her nature become, he says, that unless the grace of healing is given she will destroy herself and the kingdom with her,

> If that the heavens do not their visible spirits
> Send quickly down to tame these vile offences,
> It will come –
> Humanity must perforce prey on itself
> Like monsters of the deep.
>
> (*Lear* IV 2 46–50)

Instead of the health that was part of her birth, the inner recesses of her being now flow with poison. Her soul, conceived in love, has become twisted and disfigured by hatred.

The False King

The most be-monstered royal figure in the canon of Shakespeare's writings is Richard III. There is scarcely a sign of humanity in him. His shadow side overwhelms his conscious self. Physically he speaks of himself as 'deformed, unfinished, sent before my time into this breathing world, scarce half made up' (*Richard III* I 1 20–1). And since the heavens have shaped his body so, he says, 'let hell make crooked my mind to answer it' (*3 Henry VI* V 6 78–9). Deliberately and repeatedly in his life and relationships he chooses cruel wrong. Others describe him as 'inhuman and unnatural' with a 'hell-governed arm' (*Richard III* I 2 60, 67). He is a 'diffused infection of a man', says Lady Anne (*Richard III* I 2 78), filled with an 'interior hatred' (*Richard III* I 3 65).

Richard represents an almost total disfigurement of the king/queen archetype. In large part this perversion of royalty relates to his all-consuming lust for power. In him it knows no bounds. His brother similarly says,

> . . . for a kingdom any oath may be broken;
> I would break a thousand oaths to reign one year.
>
> (*3 Henry VI* I 2 16–17)

Power is to be sought at any cost. Richard manifests the sick soul's desperate desire to control. He is consumed by fear and a distrust of relationship. The true nature of royalty, with its willingness to take up power in order to serve the well-being of the whole realm, is in him subsumed by a compulsion to dictate because he is afraid to relate. The giving and receiving of relationship, the mutuality of opening to another, he is entirely closed to. He is deaf to the voice of mercy in his soul, prepared to murder anyone who threatens him in his insecurity. As the widow of one of his victims says, his 'murderous knife' has been sharpened on his 'stone-hard heart' (*Richard III* IV 4 228). He is the human capacity for betrayal, prepared to turn on the purest and most innocent of loves. Kissing his new-born nephew, who is an added obstruction on his path to power, Richard says in an aside,

> . . . so Judas kissed his master,
> And cried 'All hail!' when as he meant all harm.
>
> (*3 Henry VI* V 7 33–4)

The only sign of humanity that we glimpse in Richard issues up from his conscience. It surfaces in his dream life. No matter what we do to smother the voice of the soul it continues to speak, although often at levels deeper than conscious thought. In the night before battle he sees the ghosts of those whom he has murdered in the past. They sit 'heavy' in his soul like 'lead' within his bosom (*Richard III* V 3 132,153). He hears the judgement of his soul calling out, 'Guilty! Guilty!' (*Richard III* V 3 200). Upon waking Richard tries to turn from what he has heard. 'O coward conscience,' he says, 'how dost thou afflict me!' There then follows a debate within him between the true voice of his soul and the falseness of what he has become,

> What do I fear? Myself? There's none else by.
> Richard loves Richard: that is, I am I.
> Is there a murderer here? No. Yes, I am.
> Then fly. What, from myself?...
> ...Myself upon myself?
> Alack, I love myself. Wherefore? for any good
> That I myself have done unto myself?
> O, no! Alas, I rather hate myself
> For hateful deeds committed by myself.
> I am a villain. Yet I lie. I am not.
> Fool, of thyself speak well. Fool, do not flatter.
> My conscience hath a thousand several tongues,
> And every tongue brings in a several tale,
> And every tale condemns me for a villain.
>
> (*Richard III* V 3 180–96)

The debate is an argument between the true self and the false, between the goodness of what he is essentially and the evil of what he has become. It is a debate that continues in every soul. It may vary in intensity at different times and stages of life but the inner voice that calls us back to ourselves is unrelenting even though we may become adept at ignoring it.

Richard says later to one of his attendants,

> ...shadows tonight
> Have struck more terror to the soul of Richard
> Than can the substance of ten thousand soldiers.
>
> (*Richard III* V 3 217–19)

The judgement of the soul is terrifying. In the end, however, he still chooses to ignore its warnings. Instead he attempts to demean its authority,

> Conscience is but a word that cowards use,
> Devised at first to keep them strong in awe.
> Our strong arms be our conscience, swords our law!
>
> (*Richard III* V 3 310–12)

He substitutes outward power for inner truth. He sacrifices the liberty of the soul for the bondage of force. He gives way to his fears and silences the wisdom that could have given him peace.

In the evil King Richard there is no redemption because there is no love. Not only is it an absence of love for others, it is an absence of love for himself. As one of the wronged queens says of him, he is 'self-misused' (*Richard III* IV 4 375). He has violated his own soul and so violates the lives of others. He represents the way in which, when we turn against what is deepest in us, we turn against one another. A lack of love for our self leads to a lack of love for others, just as a lack of love for others will lead to a lack of true love for our self. The two are inseparably interwoven. They go hand in hand in our lives and relationships.

Richard's inhumanity separates him from true relationship and from the giving and receiving of love. His falseness covers everything in him that could be loveable. The tragic result is that he comes to believe that no one could love him,

> I shall despair. There is no creature loves me;
> And if I die, no soul shall pity me.
> Nay, wherefore should they, since that I myself
> Find in myself no pity to myself?
>
> (*Richard III* V 3 201–4)

In a sense Richard has placed himself beyond love. He represents the hellish isolation into which falseness takes us. Even at an earlier stage in his life, long before the full madness of his inhumanities, Richard had committed himself to a path of isolation,

> I have no brother, I am like no brother;
> And this word 'love', which greybeards call divine,
> Be resident in men like one another
> And not in me; I am myself alone.
>
> (*3 Henry VI* V 6 80–3)

'I am myself alone.' Richard's words anticipate the ultimate separation that he will create between himself and the rest of his kingdom. They speak of the divorce that opens up within us and between us in our lives when we sever ourselves from the root that connects us to one another and to all things.

20

While Richard remains isolated in his lack of love, King Lear, on the other hand, experiences a type of reconnection through love. Cordelia's faithfulness to him reawakens his love for her and heals some of his brokenness. When her father is still only a diminished reflection of himself, tormented in his confusions and isolation, Cordelia kneels before him and prays,

> O you kind gods,
> Cure this great breach in his abused nature!
> ... Restoration hang
> Thy medicine on my lips; and let this kiss
> Repair those violent harms that my two sisters
> Have in thy reverence made.
>
> (*Lear* IV 7 14–29)

Healing comes to Lear through love. He is reborn, but not to the superficial strength of what he was before his madness. He comes to a new depth of well-being. Physically he is weakened and now bears within himself the scars of his suffering but he is a truer person. His rebirth cannot be called a happy ending. There is still pain within him and ahead of him. He and others still pay a price for his self-inflicted sin. His redemption does not suddenly erase the wounds of ignorance. The difference, however, for Lear and for those who have been true to him is that they are connected to depths within themselves that before they knew nothing of. They are not free from suffering but they are more free from the shadow. Love has not released them from pain but it has released in them a deeper knowing and a truer seeing.

Sovereignty Reclaimed

The true sovereign is one who loves, and who knows that truthfulness in relationship is at the heart of what is first or deepest in us. As the good King Henry V says to the leaders of the nation after he has been crowned,

> ... I bid you be assured,
> I'll be your father and your brother too.
> Let me but bear your love, I'll bear your cares.
>
> (*2 Henry IV* V 2 56–8)

The king/queen archetype in us exists not in isolation but in relationship, and the health of that dimension of our being is found not in a one-way exercising of sovereignty but in a mutuality or meeting of souls.

To reach this point Henry had had to turn in his life. As he had said to his father on repenting of the misdirected energies of his earlier years,

> I shall hereafter...
> Be more myself.
>
> (*1 Henry IV* III 2 92–3)

Part of his turning around to become more truly himself involved a turning away from the superficiality of his tavern days and the self-delusions of his friends, including Sir John Falstaff, his 'fat-witted' drinking mate as he had affectionately called him (*1 Henry IV* I 2 2).

Falstaff is entirely open about his failings, endearingly so. Typically he says in his own defence that he has tried to be responsible in his life, on at least a few occasions,

> ...I was as virtuously given as a gentleman need to be.
> Virtuous enough. Swore little. Diced not above seven
> times a week. Went to a bawdy-house not above once
> in a quarter – of an hour. Paid money that I borrowed –
> three or four times. Lived well, and in good compass:
> and now I live out of all order, out of all compass.
>
> (*1 Henry IV* III 3 13–20)

Falstaff is endlessly entertaining. In large part it is because of a candid display of the sort of selfishness that is in us all. But as delightfully candid as Falstaff is, the young King Henry knows that if he is to be true to his own depths he must separate himself from the sort of falseness that the old knight represents.

At the time of his investiture to power Henry notes that Falstaff has not grasped the transition that has taken place in him from wayward prince to committed king. Falstaff is trying to exploit the new situation for his own ends, and so Henry confronts him,

> I have long dreamt of such a kind of man [as you],
> So surfeit-swelled...and so profane,
> But being awaked I do despise my dream. ....
> Presume not that I am the thing I was,
> For God doth know, so shall the world perceive,
> That I have turned away my former self;
> So will I those that kept me company.

When thou dost hear I am as I have been,
Approach me, and thou shalt be as thou wast,
The tutor and the feeder of my riots;
Till then I banish thee, on pain of death,
As I have done the rest of my misleaders,
Not to come near our person by ten mile. . . .
And as we hear you do reform yourselves,
We will, according to your strengths and qualities,
Give you advancement.

(*2 Henry IV* V 5 49–74)

These words are painful. Falstaff is a loveable character, even in the midst of his dishonesties. The pictures of eating and drinking, of merriment and exaggerated story-telling associated with him are among the most memorable in the whole canon of Shakespeare. But Henry chooses the hard path of setting a boundary for Falstaff and for what Falstaff represents in himself. 'Being awaked', as he says, Henry sees as in daylight what now he must do. Being freed from what was like the half-realization of a 'dream' he becomes conscious of what he has been choosing to ignore for too long. It is not a condemnation of the wit and humour of Falstaff, nor is it a rejection of his appetite for partying. Henry has not turned puritan. It is, however, a clear rejection of the misdirection of energies that Falstaff represents. But there is a way back. The door is not locked permanently on Falstaff. He is not being asked to become something entirely other than himself. He may return and resume a friendship with the king but it is to be within the bounds of what serves the well-being of the kingdom. It is painful but the infection needs to be cut out so that the true root of kingly relationship can flourish.

The challenge for the king/queen in us is to know exactly what the boundaries are in our lives and relationships. What needs to be cut out and what needs to be affirmed? How do we find clarity on these matters? Sometimes advisers can help us, but always there needs to be an inner attentiveness to what our soul is telling us to do. This is the role of the good counsellor, to help us consult our own depths. That is where we can weigh up the various voices of counsel. No one else can do this for us.

Henry shows such a pattern of reflection. On the night before battle we find him saying, 'I and my bosom must debate awhile' (*Henry V* IV 1 31). In solitude we can seek inner clarity, he says, and 'wash every mote' out of our conscience (*Henry V* IV 1 174–5). We can identify what is false in us in order to be reconnected to what is deeper still, the truth of our being. This does not happen in isolation from seeking the wisdom of others, but there is no substitute for the counsel of our own heart. Only thus in the face of outward opposition, as well as inward confusions, can there be a sustaining sense of the depth and direction of our inner being.

To be in touch with the root of our being frees us from over-emphasizing the branches. Acquainted with his own depths Henry views his kingship in relative terms. In the face of being surrounded by hostile French troops, he says to his threatened forces, 'We are in God's hand . . . not in theirs' (*Henry V* III 6 167). His sovereignty, like that of every life, is a derived sovereignty. Its source is deeper than us. His kingship is pure gift. It has not been achieved by him and in the end will not be saved by him. The extent to which we know our depths is the extent to which we are unimprisoned by the surface of life.

In contrast to the inner confidence of a King Henry is the obsessive fear of a false King Macbeth. Having stolen the throne of Scotland by regicide, his title 'hangs loose about him', as one of the Scottish lords says, 'like a giant's robe upon a dwarfish thief' (*Macbeth* V 2 19–22). Macbeth cannot let go of his fears because his kingship is something that he has grabbed rather than been given. He lives in perpetual anxiety of losing what is not truly his. The deepest foundations of our being are pure gift. We have not achieved them, but only received them. Our security lies not in fearfully fencing what we have taken possession of but in deeply trusting what we have been given.

The good king and queen know not only the givenness of their sovereignty, they know also the common ground from which all life springs. Speaking in disguise as an ordinary soldier, Henry V says,

> . . . I think the King is but a man, as I am: the violet
> smells to him as it doth to me; the element shows
> to him as it doth to me; all his senses have but human
> conditions. His ceremonies laid by, in his nakedness
> he appears but a man.

> (*Henry V* IV 1 99–103)

When the distinctions of life are stripped away we find a common inheritance. The whole of humanity issues up from the same ground of being. The unity is deeper than the divisions. The true king/queen in us knows that one class or category of life is not more sacred than another.

It is this type of awareness that enables a leader, as Marcus

Andronicus says, to knit together the scattered corn of a nation 'into one mutual sheaf' (*Titus* V 3 71). It builds from what is deepest rather than from what divides. It gathers the varied strands of a realm into a unity of force. Henry V calls his soldiers 'friends' and 'brothers' (*Henry V* IV Chorus 34) pointing to their commonality. He shows a reverence not only for the people of his own kingdom but for the people of every realm. Giving instructions during the English army's campaign in France, Henry says,

> . . . we give express charge, that in our marches through
> the country there be nothing compelled from the villages,
> nothing taken but paid for, none of the French upbraided
> or abused in disdainful language; for when lenity and cruelty
> play for a kingdom, the gentler gamester is the soonest
> winner.
>
> (*Henry V* III 6 105–10)

Linked inextricably with the strength and resolve of sovereignty is the type of compassion that we see practised by King Henry. 'He is gracious', as his father had said of him, and 'hath a tear for pity' (*2 Henry IV* IV 4 30–1).

No matter how powerful the king or queen is, no matter how just their vision, without mercy the life of a kingdom will not be well. There may be a type of order to it, and the realm may be held together after a fashion, but without mercy sovereignty is essentially marred. Without a willingness at the centre of the kingdom to forgive, the relationships of the realm will collapse. As Portia says in *The Merchant of Venice*, mercy is at the heart of true sovereignty,

> . . . it becomes
> The throned monarch better than his crown.
> His sceptre shows the force of temporal power. . .
> But mercy is above this sceptr'd sway;
> It is enthroned in the hearts of kings,
> It is an attribute to God himself,
> And earthly power doth then show likest God's
> When mercy seasons justice.
>
> (*Merchant* IV 1 187–97)

Many of Shakespeare's kings and queens fail. Failures in life and relationship are caused not simply by a lack of might and determination, nor simply by a loss of inner identity, but also through a lack of mercy. Whether outwardly in relation to one another or inwardly in relation to how we view and treat ourselves, a kingdom's life is undermined if there is an unwillingness to forgive. We are untrue to our own depths and to one another's depths when we refuse to be guided by mercy.

This is part of the tragedy of *Richard II*. The struggling king says,

> I had forgot myself. Am I not King?
> Awake, thou coward majesty; thou sleepest.
>
> (*Richard II* III 2 83–4)

Richard had fallen asleep to an exercising of true leadership in his kingdom, but even earlier he had fallen asleep to justice and to the way of mercy in his relationships. He had become a 'coward majesty' not just in his determination to do battle but in his desire to be merciful. To awaken the sovereignty that is within us is to become alive again to the truth of our soul's identity. It is to become attentive to the strong shepherding instinct in us that can gather into a unity the varied energies of our being. And in all of this it is to wake up to the place of grace in our souls. As Tamora, Queen of the Goths, says to her Roman captors in *Titus Andronicus*, 'mercy is nobility's true badge' (*Titus* I 1 122). Without mercy we are depleted at the very centre of the kingdom of our lives in a way that will infect every relationship that we enter. With mercy, however, we are in touch with the true core of our sovereignty where the strong foundations of relationship are built.

II

The Lover and the Friend

'Now art thou Romeo. Now art thou what thou art.'
(Romeo and Juliet II 4 87–8)

The True Lover and Friend

Like the primordial archetypes of king and queen, images of the lover and friend come down to us from the earliest times. They appear in prehistoric legend and art-form like the characters that visit us in our dreams or in the timeless fairytale realm of love-trysts and betrayals. The lover and the friend are deep in the core of our inner being. They are expressions of an ancient pattern in the human mystery.

The archetypes of lover and friend represent that part of our soul that we can know only in relationship. We approach whole-ness in our lives not in isolation but in relation. There are dimensions within us that are awakened into consciousness only through the experience of love and friendship, or through the longings for love and friendship that stir within us.

The lover in us desires to give and receive from the centre of our being, to share with another the secrets of the self and its hidden yearnings. It is that dimension of us that longs to fully trust another and to relate in nakedness, both physically and spiritually. It seeks to be stripped of the coverings that separate us. The lover desires union. It is that part of us that can make the other feel most wanted and ultimately cherished.

The friend similarly seeks mutuality in the giving and receiving of relationship. There is a delight in the other's presence and the experience of being at home in one another's company. The friend in our soul wants what is best for the other, including wanting the other to have many friends. It is that part of us in relationship that sees with generosity, but not with naivety. The friend wants to be faithful to what is true.

The reality, of course, for most of us much of the time is that we live at a distance from the true depths of the lover and the friend. We choose not to open wide the inner chamber of our hearts, even to those who have most loved us. Sometimes this is because we believe the other lacks the capacity to delight in our true self. Usually, however, it is because we are afraid to open our soul. The fear is related either to rejections that we have suffered in the past or to our own reluctance to face what is within us, or both. Yet it is only as we allow the energies of

29

relationship to shed further light on the inner landscape of our lives that we will move towards a greater self-clarity.

The depths of the lover and friend are awakened by relationship or by the longings for relationship that are born within us. In *As You Like It* Orlando, upon meeting Rosalind, says that he has been 'love-shaked' (*As You* III 2 352). Her presence has set loose the lover in him. He is aware of a new surging of energy. It shakes free part of his inner being. Similarly Julia in *The Two Gentlemen of Verona* refers to 'the inly touch of love' (*Gentlemen* II 7 18). It releases a flow in the depths of the human soul. To be awakened to our longings for love is to be more fully alive. As Mercutio observes after Romeo and Juliet have set each other alight, 'Now art thou Romeo. Now art thou what thou art' (*Romeo* II 4 87–8). In love he has become not something other than himself but more truly himself. And it is not on his own that Romeo has become more authentically Romeo. It is in relation to Juliet that the face of his soul more truly emerges. Love brings to life in us depths that we would not otherwise know.

An awakening to the lover within ourselves gives rise also to an awareness that the stream of love that carries us is deeper and broader than our particular longings and expressions of love. It is coursing through us but its origins are before us and its current is mightier than anything of our own creating. Juliet says to Romeo,

> My bounty is as boundless as the sea,
> My love as deep. The more I give to thee,
> The more I have, for both are infinite.
>
> (*Romeo* II 2 133–5)

The experience is of a force running through us that is at the same time greater than us. We have not chosen love. Love has chosen us. We have not decided to fall in love. Rather we find ourselves in love.

Love opens the eyes of our hearts to a realm that is deeper than anything that separates us. In the case of Romeo and Juliet, it is deeper than the 'cankered hate' that exists between their respective families, the warring Montagues and Capulets (*Romeo* I 1 95). Love partakes of the unity that precedes life's divisions. It releases us from the tightly drawn boundaries that culture and religion or race and class have erected. We are set free from the definitions that lock us into opposition against one another. Juliet sees Romeo not primarily as a Montague but as himself.

His family name is an enemy to her family but, as she says of her lover, he cannot be captured by outward definition:

> What's in a name? that which we call a rose
> By any other name would smell as sweet.
> So Romeo would, were he not Romeo called,
> Retain that dear perfection which he owes
> Without that title. Romeo, doff thy name;
> And for that name which is no part of thee,
> Take all myself.
>
> (*Romeo* II 2 43–9)

It is the lover in us that asks the question, 'What's in a name?', for the lover knows life at levels deeper than outward categories. The lover is closer to the heart of life than the hater.

The tragedy of Romeo and Juliet is caused not by a failure in the lovers but by a blindness in the haters. The Montagues and the Capulets have set fixed boundaries on the distinctions of life. They have allowed their differences to obscure the common root that feeds and sustains them both. And the less they see what unites them the more they accentuate what divides them. The result is the tragic death of the lovers. This is the way of hatred. It not only consumes those who hate but wounds those who love. The innocent are caught in the web of wrong and violation. Over the dead bodies of Romeo and Juliet, the old Capulet grieves. They are the 'poor sacrifices of our enmity', he says (*Romeo* V 3 304). They knew a love that was deeper than their family hatreds. They knew it in their bodies and in their souls, and, although their deaths are like a sacrifice that begins to heal the brokenness of their families, it is their knowing of love that leads to their suffering. There is always a cost to the waking of the lover in us. It calls for self-giving within. It can lead also to conflicts from without.

Romeo and Juliet die. Even though their love had made them more alive, their family hatreds shape their tragic end. Love had brought them into a union stronger than death but family bitterness kills them. The lover and the hater move in opposite directions in our souls. Hatred tears us apart. Love, on the other hand, as Hermia says in *A Midsummer Night's Dream*, is 'that which knitteth souls' together (*Midsummer* I 1 172). It weaves into one fabric the depths of the lover and the beloved, just as it conjoins their bodies and combines their possessions. The good King Henry V says to his future bride, the daughter of the King of France, 'Kate, when France is mine, and I am yours, then yours is France, and you are mine'

(*Henry V* V 2 174–5). To be awakened to the lover in us is to move more deeply towards the interrelationship and the sharing of life. As lovers we know that we do not exist in isolated individuality. The interwovenness that we experience in love is an expression of the interdependency of all things. In love we are further opened to this mystery and strengthened to see one another and to see all things not in separation but in relationship.

The lover wants to share with the beloved. Their souls are intermingled. They are like two parts of a whole. When Romeo hears Juliet's voice he says, 'It is my soul that calls upon my name' (*Romeo* II 2 164). It is as if she speaks to him from within. But love is not simply a sharing or intermingling. It is also a discovering and creating together of what has not been known before. It is a being drawn further into the night, or into the unknown, through an interflowing or intercourse of our beings. Juliet invokes the night and its darkness so that 'strange love', as she calls it, the energies for love in her that she does not yet know, or of which she is unsure, may 'grow bold':

> Come, night. Come, Romeo. Come, thou day in night;
> For thou wilt lie upon the wings of night
> Whiter than new snow on a raven's back.
> Come, gentle night. Come, loving, black-browed night.
> Give me my Romeo. And when I shall die,
> Take him and cut him out in little stars,
> And he will make the face of heaven so fine
> That all the world will be in love with night
> And pay no worship to the garish sun.
>
> (*Romeo* III 2 17–25)

The lover in us seeks what the mystics call the realm of 'unknowing'. It is a type of knowing or relating associated with the night rather than with the light of day. It is a deep knowing – intuitive, mystical, sensuous – rather than an analytical or reasoned knowing at the surface of life's relationships.

The intimate knowing that is experienced by Romeo and Juliet is primarily that of the lover, but they are also friends. Juliet calls Romeo her 'love-lord' as well as her 'husband-friend' (*Romeo* III 5 43). The energies of the lover and friend in us overlap. In the richest of loves they coexist, but they are distinct energies. At the simplest of levels the friend can be described as one with whom we like to 'waste the time together', as Portia says in *The Merchant of Venice* (*Merchant* III 4 11). It is the simple delight in one another's presence. It is that part of us that feels better in the company of the other.

At a more intentional level, however, the friend is one whom we seek out. At some level within ourselves we know that well-being lies in relationship. In *Hamlet* Polonius advises his son Laertes to 'grapple them to your soul with hoops of steel' (*Hamlet* I 3 63). To be well in our souls is to nurture the bonds of friendship. To seek wholeness in our inner being is to be attentive to our longings for relationship. Our soul-friends, or the 'friends of my soul' as Albany calls them in *King Lear* (*Lear* V 3 317), are a vital part of coming to know who we are. The friend of the soul is one to whom we show what is within us, hiding nothing, revealing everything. Duke Orsino in *Twelfth Night* says to his friend,

> Thou knowest no less but all. I have unclasped
> To thee the book even of my secret soul.
>
> (*Twelfth* I 4 13–14)

It is in trying to open our 'secret soul' to the other that we begin to read more clearly the text of our inner selves. The knowledge of our self happens not in isolation but in the interminglings of relationship. In friendship, as in love, we become more aware of the interconnectedness of life. In *The Two Noble Kinsmen* Hippolyta, Queen of the Amazons, says that friendship reveals to us a knotwork in which the strands of our lives are interwoven. And concerning her husband Theseus, she says that he 'cannot be umpire to himself' (*Kinsmen* I 3 45). Without opening to another the gateway of our inner self we cannot clearly judge what is within us. It is as we disclose the longings and the turmoil of our soul to another that we come to a clearer knowing of the energies that are pulsating in our depths.

Comic Failure in Love and Friendship

As with the other archetypes it is easier to point to what the lover and the friend are not than to describe what they truly are. Failures in love and friendship are countless. They are more plentiful in our lives and often more colourful than our successes. We know more about flaws than perfections in relationship. The journey towards true love and friendship takes us through failure. Sometimes these experiences are painful and cruel. At other points they are ridiculous and absurd.

There is the far too intense lover described by Jaques in *As You*

Like It, 'sighing like furnace, with a woeful ballad made to his mistress' eyebrow' (*As You* II 7 149–50). Sometimes the passion that stirs within us misses the mark in life. Rather than taking us closer to the heart of the other, and making us more alive, we spin with misdirected longings that end up dissipating the energies of our soul. At such times the true hunger of the lover in us has not been identified. Nor has it been satisfied.

At other times we miss the soul of others by getting stuck at not liking their bodies. In *The Comedy of Errors*, a story of confused identities, one of the Dromio twins is mistakenly claimed by the wrong woman, or by what he calls 'the mountain of mad flesh that claims marriage of me' (*Comedy* IV 4 152–3). He sees only her exterior, as his account to his master makes clear,

> Marry, sir, she's the kitchen wench, and all grease;
> and I know not what use to put her to but to make a
> lamp of her and run from her by her own light. I
> warrant her rags and the tallow in them will burn a
> Poland winter. If she lives till doomsday she'll
> burn a week longer than the whole world.
>
> (*Comedy* III 2 98–103)

She is 'spherical, like a globe', he says, in which whole countries can be found. Ireland, for instance, he identifies 'in her buttocks' because of 'the bogs'. Spain he is not able to see, but feels 'hot in her breath'. The Indies he discovers on her nose, 'all o'er embellished with rubies, carbuncles, sapphires'. And the Netherlands he is not able to find at all because, as he explains, he 'did not look so low' (*Comedy* III 2 120f.).

We laugh because we know how funny the human body can be, and because we know that sometimes we too have been judged by our shape or by the size of particular parts of our anatomy. Comedy enables us to laugh at such experience, even though at times it has been hurtful. It opens us to seeing things anew, to seeing the absurdity, for instance, of measuring another human being in terms of their exterior. Comedy challenges us by playing with our superficial prejudices to cut through to deeper ways of perceiving. Nothing can be truly viewed in mere isolation or simply as an object. Everything exists in a web of interrelationship.

That part of us that desires to live in relationship, and knows that the truest encounters of life happen at levels deeper than the surface, is easily obscured when we focus limitedly on the outward. Sometimes we get stuck at not liking the body of another.

At other times the fixation is of an exaggerated attraction to specific parts of the body, and we again end up missing the soul. Parolles in *All's Well That Ends Well* fastens on to the sexual. Advising the chaste Helena to give away her virginity, he views it more in physical terms than in relational terms. Comically he argues that there is little to be said for keeping it,

> ... 'tis against the rule of nature. To speak on the
> part of virginity is to accuse your mothers, which
> is most infallible disobedience.
>
> *(All's Well* I 1 134–7)

Virginity is like a valuable 'commodity', he contends, but as an object of desire it loses its value with time. 'The longer kept, the less worth', he says. 'Old virginity is like one of our French withered pears: it looks ill, it eats drily; marry, 'tis a withered pear' *(All's Well* I 1 152–60).

Parolles gives voice to our obsession with the sexual and to the common prejudice that the older the body the less valuable. He expresses our shadow tendency to turn the sexual into an object, like a 'commodity', as if our bodies existed independently of our souls. The lover, on the other hand, knows that true sexuality is an expression of a deeper reality. It is a gift freely given in the mutuality of relationship. The lover in us also knows that the depth of sexual encounter corresponds to the depth of the relationship, and that delight is commensurate with trust.

We miss the centre of another, as well as our own centre, when the shadow of the lover or friend dominates. Especially when we turn in on ourselves instead of following the outward movement of the soul, we become trapped. In self-absorption we fail to notice the deep yearning in us for self-giving. We become blind to the inner truth that it is in sharing our self that we find our self, that it is in giving our self away in love that we most deeply secure the foundations of our self. Malvolio the steward in *Twelfth Night*, who at the deepest of levels longs for intimacy in relationship but who in practice isolates himself, gives the impression, as one of the other servants says, that he is proud and 'best persuaded of himself' *(Twelfth* II 3 142). The reality is that he is least persuaded of himself. So unsure is he of his own centre that he compulsively spends time gazing at his own image, desperately trying to locate the beauty of his being. As the same servant says of him, 'he has been yonder i'the sun practising behaviour to his own shadow this half-hour' *(Twelfth* II 5 16–17). It is a picture of life passing him by and of missing the relationships of life. He is standing in the sunlight but is entirely unaware of those around him, so imprisoned is he on focusing on himself. Yet he will not find his true self by gazing at his shadow for his shadow-side has been captured by the fantasy of thinking that he will be the master of the house, dominating rather than sharing in relationship. He is not in touch with others. Nor is he truly in touch with himself.

When the extent of Malvolio's self-inflation is exposed by other members of the household, his response to them is,

> Go, hang yourselves all. You are idle, shallow
> things; I am not of your element.
>
> (*Twelfth* III 4 122–3)

He fails in his relationship with others because he has failed in his relationship with himself, and he cuts himself off from his own depths because he has cut himself off from others. Failing to recognize the true longings for relationship that are present in his own soul, and failing to see that these longings are deep within every human being, he moves further into isolation. His words, 'I am not of your element', seal his self-imprisonment. They further distance him from others as well as from his own depths.

Shakespeare's most colourful character of failure in relationship is Sir John Falstaff. We find him in *1 Henry VI* fleeing from a scene of battle in order to save his own skin. When asked if he will really abandon his leader, Lord Talbot, Falstaff responds, 'Ay, all the Talbots in the world, to save my life' (*1 Henry VI* III 2 108). He is candid about his selfishness. He comically says what most of us think much of the time but usually are too inhibited to say. Yet his openness does not express a willingness to engage in relationship in a way that might alter him. It is simply a bald statement of isolated individuality. Falstaff thinks he can save himself by abandoning others and that his own well-being can be achieved with no regard to friendship. In a limited sense he is right, and to a certain extent he gets away with it by employing humour. Inviting laughter at his selfish candour he cleverly side-steps the need to change. In excusing himself to Prince Hal, he says, 'Thou seest I have more flesh than another man, and therefore more frailty' (*1 Henry IV* III 3 165–6). Our shadow-side is adept at hiding from the true nature of relationship. Sometimes we use humour. At other points we use circumstance or personal weakness and illness. Our ego is infinitely capable of finding excuses in the conscious realm for patterns of behaviour which at a deeper level we know are inexcusable. Our own well-being is ultimately linked to one another's well-being. We cannot truly be well within ourselves if we are violating the archetype of the friend in our soul.

In *The Merry Wives of Windsor* we find Falstaff trying to seduce married women in order to secure their wealth. His unsuccessful attempt on Mistress Page produces the determination in her, as she says, 'to exhibit a bill in the parliament for the putting down of men' (*Merry* II 1 26–7). Mistress Ford similarly responds to Falstaff's disingenuousness by warning her friend, 'I will find you twenty lascivious turtles ere one chaste man' (*Merry* II 1 75). In revenge the women arrange for Falstaff to have to hide in a laundry basket to escape being caught and beaten by their husbands. The servants then dump the laundry basket into the river. Typically Falstaff shows no remorse. Instead, in his subsequent account of the escapade, he digresses into his favourite diversion, humour. He says to his friend,

> You may know by my size that I have a kind of alacrity
> in sinking. . . . The water swells a man, and what a
> thing should I have been when I had been swelled!
> I should have been a mountain of mummy.
>
> (*Merry* III 5 10–16)

Falstaff is incorrigible. 'If my wind were but long enough to say my prayers,' he says, 'I would repent' (*Merry* III 5 93). But he does not repent. In fact he shows no inclination to change at all. It is as if the long practice of treating others merely as the means to his own pleasure has made him unaware of the deeper desires for relationship in the human soul. If he does hear the counsel of his own heart, and its guidance towards truthfulness and its warnings against falseness, he makes light even of this. 'I think the devil will not have me damned,' he says, 'lest the oil that's in me should set hell on fire' (*Merry* V 5 34–5).

Falstaff is irresistibly amusing, and we identify with him in his pursuit of pleasure and his avoidance of conscience, but in the end his selfishness is intolerable. His false patterns have to be rejected. Caught out once too many times, his betrayal of relationship, especially in the battlefield, is named for what it is. The king speaks in judgement against him,

> Stain to thy countrymen, thou hearest thy doom.
> Be packing therefore, thou that wast a knight;
> Henceforth we banish thee on pain of death.
>
> (*1 Henry VI* IV 1 45–7)

'Thou that wast a knight.' His outward behaviour had come to bear no relationship to the inner reality of knighthood, and so he is stripped of his title. His falseness costs him the company of those he had enjoyed. Faithlessness has no ultimate future in relationship. In the end there is no place for it except exile.

Tragic Failure in Love and Friendship

Many of our outward failures in relationship are caused by an inner betrayal of our soul. As one of the French Lords in *All's Well That Ends Well* says, we are 'our own traitors' (*All's Well* IV 3 20). We set in motion a collapse of our relationships when we are untrue to our own depths or when we do not know our own depths. In the tragedy of *Troilus and Cressida* Cressida vows that the foundations of her love are immovable, 'like the very centre of the earth' (*Troilus* IV 2 103). All it takes for her to be shaken in her love for Troilus, however, is a change of location. A shift from Troy to the Greek camp outside the besieged city is accompanied also by a shift in her affections. As she says of Troilus in soliloquy, 'one eye yet looks on thee' (*Troilus* V 2 109). With her other eye, however, she is already looking elsewhere. Her need for love is strong, but her foundations for relationship are shaky. So unsure is she of her own centre that her excursions into love are confused.

Troilus witnesses her faithlessness and his words convey the pain of being betrayed. 'Cressid is mine,' he says, 'tied with the bonds of heaven.' But the agonizing realization in him is that 'the bonds of heaven are slipped, dissolved' (*Troilus* V 2 156–8). The union of body and soul that he had experienced as everlasting is broken. The love that seemed beyond corruption lies in ruins. The human capacity for faithlessness, the shadow lover in us, suddenly rears its head and smashes to pieces what before seemed indissoluble. The true lover and the false lover are never far apart in us. They are like cousins, and when we forget their relationship we are especially prone to the destructive energies of the shadow.

Troilus and Cressida is a tragedy of betrayal. The tragedy of *Antony and Cleopatra*, on the other hand, is a story not of faithlessness but of a devotion in relationship that ends up consuming the lovers. Antony and Cleopatra allow the energies of the lover to overwhelm them. The other dimensions of their soul are suppressed. It is as if the king/queen archetype is entirely absent. The shadow lover overpowers the sovereign. Antony and Cleopatra allow the lover to become the dictator and it destroys them.

This is not to deny the beauty of their passion. As Cleopatra says, 'Eternity was in our lips and eyes' (*Antony* I 3 35). In love they have tasted the union that is deeper than the separation of time and space. They have glimpsed a boundlessness in their self-giving. Cleopatra wondering whether there can be any definition to their experience of love, Antony replies, 'Then must thou needs find out new heaven, new earth' (*Antony* I 1 17). It is beyond the categories of what outwardly can be known. It partakes of the realm of unknowing, or the world of inner knowing that cannot be measured in recognizable forms.

And yet there is something destructively insatiable in Cleopatra's appetite for love. Every other dimension of her being is enslaved to the lover in her. Every ounce of her vitality is poured into what is like a desperation of loving. As Antony says to her,

> Though you can guess what temperance should be,
> You know not what it is.
>
> (*Antony* III 13 121–2)

She allows her need and longings for love to become a tyrant in her soul. It refuses to be checked by any other balance and it consumes her.

Antony realizes that he must break off 'from this enchanting queen', as he calls her (*Antony* I 2 129). The tension between intellect and emotion, and between the rational and the sensuous, symbolized by the differences between Rome and the western world on the one hand, and, on the other hand, Egypt and the mystical intuitive world of the east, is lost. Cleopatra is all emotion, all sensuousness. Antony, the Roman soldier *par excellence*, says,

> These strong Egyptian fetters I must break,
> Or lose myself in dotage.
>
> (*Antony* I 2 117–18)

But he cannot tear himself away. The passion of the lover in him now assumes total control. It displaces the other energies of his soul, including the warrior. He loses the sharpness of his reasoned judgement and military precision. During a sea battle, at the height of the conflict just as the battle is turning in Antony's direction, Cleopatra flees and Antony follows. His fleet of ships is ruined.

Furious at how the strength of the soldier in him has been weakened by his all-consuming love, Antony accuses Cleopatra,

> Egypt, thou knew'st too well
> My heart was to thy rudder tied by th'strings,
> And thou shouldst tow me after. . . .
> . . . You did know
> How much you were my conqueror; and that
> My sword, made weak by my affection, would
> Obey it on all cause.
>
> (*Antony* III 11 56–68)

He has allowed the shadow lover in him to undermine his strength and direction of soul. Like the shadow of every other archetype it has the capacity to diminish us. The true lover makes us more fully ourselves. The false lover makes Antony less than himself.

Antony loving her but hating the debilitating 'fetters' of their love, and Cleopatra loving him but being consumed by the distractions of her passion, the relationship destroys them both. Overwhelmed by his military opponents, Antony falls on his sword to end his life, although even this he is unable to do with precision. In his last moments he calls out to Cleopatra, 'I am dying, Egypt, dying' (*Antony* IV 15 18). The tragedy for Antony is that all along parts of him had been dying because of the shadow lover in him. All along there were true depths in his soul that were being suffocated by the overpowering confusions of their relationship.

Upon the death of Antony, Cleopatra too lays plans to take her life. Holding a poisonous asp to her breast she says,

> . . . Come, thou mortal wretch,
> With thy sharp teeth this knot intrinsicate
> Of life at once untie.
>
> (*Antony* V 2 302–4)

The tragedy for Cleopatra is that all along in the relationship a true integration of soul was being untied in her. Her obsessive passion for Antony was unravelling the threads of her queenship. So distant had she become from a sovereign relationship with her realm that she lived as if there were no future apart from Antony. The shadow lover had deceived her into believing that life could have no meaning without him. Instead of the gift of love further awakening her to the richness of life's relationships, the shadow of love had blinded her to everything except the beauty of Antony. Rather than expanding her passions for life it had contracted her focus onto a single path that ends tragically.

Another character capable of great love and friendship who in the end destroys himself is Brutus in *Julius Caesar*. The tragedy is born out of Brutus' betrayal of his own depths. His sense of self is weak and he becomes prone to the manipulation of others. It is true that we come to know ourselves through one another. There are certain perspectives that we cannot gain on our own. As Brutus says to his friend Cassius, 'the eye sees not itself but by reflection' (*Julius* I 2 52–3). But we need also to look with our own eyes. Brutus lacks a strength of inner perspective and his weakness is exploited. Cassius begins by saying to him,

> . . . I, your glass,
> Will modestly discover to yourself
> That of yourself which you yet know not of.
>
> (*Julius* I 2 68–70)

Initially Brutus is cautious of where Cassius is leading him,

> Into what dangers would you lead me, Cassius,
> That you would have me seek into myself
> For that which is not in me?
>
> (*Julius* I 2 63–5)

But more and more he is tempted by the flattering exaggeration of Cassius' descriptions, especially by the comparison between his greatness and Caesar's greatness. 'Why should that name be sounded more than yours?', asks Cassius (*Julius* I 2 142). And so Brutus finds himself wanting to believe the assertion of the anonymous letter thrown in at his window, 'Brutus, thou sleep'st: awake, and see thyself' (*Julius* II 1 46). The letter contains half-truths. Brutus is asleep to aspects of his own person. He does not clearly see himself. The temptation, however, moves him towards an inflated sense of self. It stirs him, but not towards true wakefulness. Rather it carries him towards delusion.

Even so, Brutus continues for a while to be attentive to his conscience. At first he resists the suggestion of conspiracy against Caesar. Noticing the effect of Cassius' words on his soul, Brutus in soliloquy says,

> Since Cassius first did whet me against Caesar,
> I have not slept.
>
> (*Julius* II 1 61–2)

He is alert to the way in which a betrayal of friendship sets in motion a turmoil of the soul. At such moments, he says,

> ... the state of man,
> Like to a little kingdom, suffers then
> The nature of an insurrection.
>
> (*Julius* II 1 67–9)

We find ourselves torn in our depths when we are tempted to be false to the spirit of friendship and to the important relationships of our lives.

Brutus continues for a time to be wary of Cassius and the other conspirators. They visit him in the night with their faces hidden. Brutus knows within himself that such secrecy signals falsehood,

> ... O conspiracy,
> Sham'st thou to show thy dangerous brow by night,
> When evils are most free? O then, by day
> Where wilt thou find a cavern dark enough
> To mask thy monstrous visage?
>
> (*Julius* II 1 77–80)

Yet he ignores these inner warnings. He chooses also to ignore the insights of his wife Portia, who knows that something is not well within him,

> It will not let you eat, nor talk, nor sleep;
> And could it work so much upon your shape,
> As it hath much prevailed on your condition,
> I should not know you Brutus. Dear my lord,
> Make me acquainted with your cause of grief.
>
> (*Julius* II 1 252–6)

Without knowing of the conspiracy she senses in his mind a 'sick offence', as she calls it, and begs Brutus,

> By all your vows of love, and that great vow
> Which did incorporate and make us one,
> That you unfold to me, your self, your half,
> Why you are so heavy, and what men tonight
> Have had resort to you; for here have been
> Some six or seven, who did hide their faces
> Even from darkness.
>
> (*Julius* II 1 272–8)

Brutus is imprisoned by his shadow. He cannot open his heart even to the one who loves him, to the one who is like his 'self' or 'half'. His closure to her is an expression of his closure to himself. He cannot let her in to his inner turmoil because he is not allowing himself to truly confront the struggle in his soul. Portia responds by asking,

> ... Am I your self
> But, as it were, in sort or limitation,
> To keep with you at meals, comfort your bed,
> And talk to you sometimes? Dwell I but in the suburbs
> Of your good pleasure? If it be no more,
> Portia is Brutus' harlot, not his wife.
>
> (*Julius* II 1 282–7)

Her question, 'Dwell I but in the suburbs of your good pleasure?', speaks as much of what Brutus is doing to himself as of what he is doing to her. When we push those close to us away from our depths we are also distancing ourselves from our true centre. We are choosing to ignore the inner messages of truth.

Brutus follows the twisted counsel of Cassius and more and more separates himself from his own soul. He attempts to justify his betrayal of friendship and deceives himself into believing that there are different types of murder, some acceptable and others damnable. To the conspirators he says,

> Let's kill him boldly, but not wrathfully;
> Let's carve him as a dish fit for the gods,
> Not hew him as a carcass fit for hounds.
>
> (*Julius* II 1 172–4)

And when they have assassinated Caesar, Brutus declares,

> ... let us bathe our hands in Caesar's blood
> Up to the elbows, and besmear our swords;
> Then walk we forth, even to the market-place,
> And waving our red weapons o'er our heads,
> Let's all cry, 'Peace, freedom and liberty!'
>
> (*Julius* III 1 106–10)

Brutus has fooled himself into believing that the killing of a friend could possibly produce 'peace, freedom and liberty'. The reality is a violence that will in turn beget violence, a bondage to delusion, and an imprisonment to his shadow. When we are false to our own soul we breed wrongs and confusions around us in our lives.

In the market-place Brutus continues in his self-delusion when he says,

> . . . If there be any in this assembly, any dear friend of
> Caesar's, to him I say that Brutus' love to Caesar
> was no less than his. If then that friend demand
> why Brutus rose against Caesar, this is my answer:
> not that I loved Caesar less, but that I loved Rome
> more. . . . As Caesar loved me, I weep for him; as
> he was fortunate, I rejoice at it; as he was valiant,
> I honour him; but, as he was ambitious, I slew him.
>
> (*Julius* III 2 17–26)

Brutus, blind to the cravings of his own shadow, projects his ambitious desires onto Caesar. And long before he does violence to Caesar he has done violence to his own soul and to the integrity of his own faculty of reasoning. The false deed that springs out of his unnamed and unrecognized desire for self-aggrandizement he claims to be for the well-being of the nation.

In the end the crowd and the senate turn against Brutus' falseness and he is forced to flee from Rome, living as a fugitive from his home and from his wife. It is an outward banishment that reflects the inner exile that already has taken place in Brutus' soul. Having betrayed his own depths he lives in an imprisonment to his shadow. He wanders restlessly, and in his sleepless nights he is visited by a ghost that calls itself Brutus' 'evil spirit' (*Julius* IV 3 279). His shadow side haunts his nights and consumes his days. In the end he takes his life.

Although Brutus betrays the archetype of the friend in his own depths he does not in fact lose all capacity for friendship, nor does he lose the desire for relationship that is deep in the human mystery. Indeed, part of what consumes him is his grief at the death of Portia. In the tragedy of *Timon of Athens*, however, Timon falls out of touch with this dimension of the soul. He cuts himself off from his own desire for relationship. He represents that tendency in us to become bitter when wronged and to retreat into isolation. Timon had not known himself well enough to know also what was in others. Denying the shadow in his own depths he had been unwise to how it might appear in those around him. Blind to the way in which light and dark are variously woven together in the human spirit, he suspected nothing of what was underneath the surface of his 'varnished friends' (*Timon* IV 2 36). When Timon was wealthy they were willing to offer him the guise of friendship. When he lost his wealth, however, they deserted him. Having been naive to the shadow side of the human he becomes bitter in the extreme. Having at some level chosen not to see the selfish preoccupations of those who benefited from him in the past but who now were unwilling to help him, Timon cries out,

> ...O see the monstrousness of man
> When he looks out in an ungrateful shape.
>
> (*Timon* III 2 74–5)

It is when we are least aware of the shadows in our own depths that we are most shaken by the falseness of others.

Timon decides to withdraw entirely from human contact. In the pain of his bitterness he says,

> Timon will to the woods, where he shall find
> Th'unkindest beast more kinder than mankind.
>
> (*Timon* IV 1 35–6)

Then in a perverted utterance of devotion he prays,

> And grant, as Timon grows, his hate may grow
> To the whole race of mankind, high and low. Amen.
>
> (*Timon* IV 1 39–40)

As the fool later says of Timon, his nature has been 'infected' (*Timon* IV 3 203). The face of his soul is distorted by the wrongs that he has suffered. He calls himself 'Misanthropos', a hater of humanity (*Timon* IV 3 54). It is an expression of the human soul recoiling in the face of wrongdoing and hurt. In the end it destroys him. It more deeply harms his soul than the initial faithlessness of his friends. Desperate to build a hard protective shell around himself, eventually his soul is suffocated.

Even in the midst of his hateful bitterness, however, we catch a final glimpse of Timon's true depths peeking out. When Flavius, his faithful steward, comes to the wood offering to share with him the little bit of wealth that he had saved over his years of service, Timon says, 'one honest man' (*Timon* IV 3 489). This brief opening to another human being, however, does not last long. His soul again quickly covers over with doubt. He suspects his steward's generosity. 'That which I show, heaven knows, is merely love,' says Flavius (*Timon* IV 3 518). But acts of 'mere love'

45

are suspect when our hearts have been hardened by betrayal in relationship. Timon's soul is closed off. He cannot believe the candid simplicity of Flavius' expression of love.

Timon is shut in on himself and, with the exception of the one fleeting glimpse of openness towards his steward, he is closed to change. This is one of the marks of hatred's infection. It makes us resist transformation. It undermines the natural pattern of giving and receiving in relationship. Don John, the embittered brother of the Prince of Arragon in *Much Ado About Nothing*, out of sheer spite seeks to destroy what is good and beautiful in other people's relationships. He says, 'let me be that I am, and seek not to alter me' (*Much Ado* I 3 33–4). His words speak of the death of relationship. They speak of the hardening of the human soul when it goes down the path of bitterness.

The Anti-type of Relationship

Similarly Iago in *Othello* is closed to redemptive change. He is the anti-type of love and friendship. Even his name 'Iago' is a fragmented version of *Imago*. He represents a perversion of the sacred image, the *Imago Dei* in the human spirit. He is a distortion of the original pattern of the soul with its desires for relationship. And whereas Timon is open in his expressions of hurt and hatred, Iago is hidden and deceitful. Outwardly he is regarded as a man of 'exceeding honesty' (*Othello* III 3 255) and 'trust' (*Othello* I 3 282) but inwardly, as he says in soliloquy, 'I am not what I am' (*Othello* I 1 66). Not only does he live far from his true self, but his false self is hidden from view. It is like a double falseness in him. He does not know his true centre, or the heart of any other human being. He does know, however, that he wants to conceal his shadow side.

Iago suspects what is deepest and most natural in the human spirit. In his mind love, with its sexual expressions, is turned into mere bestiality. In reporting that Othello the Moor and Desdemona have eloped, he says to her father,

> Even now, now, very now, an old black ram
> Is tupping your white ewe.
>
> (*Othello* I 1 89–90)

He projects on to others his twisted perceptions of relationship. His own confused sexual energies he reads into everyone else's actions, reducing the passion of love to mere animality. For Iago human nature, including our physical nature, is essentially perverted. Within us, as he contends in a dialogue about love, is a baseness that only can be held in check by the will:

> Our bodies are our gardens, to the which our wills
> are gardeners. ... If the beam of our lives had not
> one scale of reason to poise another of sensuality,
> the blood and baseness of our natures would conduct
> us to most preposterous conclusions. But we
> have reason to cool our raging motions, our
> carnal stings, our unbitted lusts: whereof I take
> this, that you call love, to be a sect or scion. ...
> It is merely a lust of the blood and a permission
> of the will.
>
> (*Othello* I 3 316–32)

Love, the deepest expression of the soul's desire for relationship, Iago turns into a mere 'lust of the blood'. He sees others in terms of his own sickness. The more distant we become from the true depths of our being the less we believe these depths are in others. And the less we believe these depths are in others the more we will treat them with disrespect.

It is not clear what has so distorted the soul of Iago, and we do not know what his experiences of love have been. We do know, however, that within his own marriage the initial attraction to his wife has been lost. Again Iago projects his own state of soul onto others. Desdemona, he says, will inevitably tire of Othello and look elsewhere for sexual gratification. When he sees her innocently taking the hand of Othello's friend Cassio, he calls it a sign of her 'lechery' (*Othello* II 1 249). Similarly, with no foundation in truth, he suspects Othello of having slept with his wife, Emilia:

> ... I do suspect the lusty Moor
> Hath leaped into my seat, the thought whereof
> Doth, like a poisonous mineral, gnaw my inwards,
> And nothing can, or shall, content my soul
> Till I am evened with him, wife for wife;
> Or failing so, yet that I put the Moor
> At least into a jealousy so strong
> That judgement cannot cure.
>
> (*Othello* II 1 286–93)

Fears and suspicions have eaten away at the soul of Iago. He is paranoid in his relationships and blind to the goodness that is in others.

Even when Iago manages to see beauty in another, he sees it as a threat to his own being. Concerning Cassio he says,

> He hath a daily beauty in his life
> That makes me ugly.
>
> (*Othello* V 1 19–20)

When we are out of touch with the beauty of our own being we feel intimidated by beauty in others. When we operate from ill-will and an ugliness of motive in our own hearts we feel judged by the generosity of spirit and clarity of will that we witness in the relationships of others.

And so Iago sets out to twist what is beautiful in those around him. 'Divinity of hell!', he calls it (*Othello* II 3 340), the perverting of what is good, the swallowing up of what has its origins in heaven. As the plotting of evil begins to hatch in his mind, he says of Desdemona,

> So will I turn her virtue into pitch,
> And out of her own goodness make the net
> That shall enmesh them all.
>
> (*Othello* II 3 350–2)

Having lost contact with his own goodness, he sets out to destroy it in others. Having been perverted in his own soul, he attempts to use what is healthiest in those around him for their eventual ill. All of this he does under the cloak of deceit. To Othello he says, 'My lord, you know I love you' (*Othello* III 3 116), echoing the biblical words of the disciple Peter who betrayed his master. And with clear resonances of the phrase 'all will be well, all manner of things shall be well' from St Julian of Norwich's fourteenth-century *Revelations of Divine Love*, Iago says to the distraught Desdemona, 'all things shall be well' (*Othello* IV 2 170). What Iago in fact intends is that all things shall be hell. The chaos of his own soul he attempts to recreate in the world around him. It is the attempt to visit upon others the turmoil of his own inner realm.

Iago's deceit is based initially on a sowing of doubt in Othello. 'Look to your wife,' he says, 'observe her well with Cassio' (*Othello* III 3 195). Suspicions are planted that have no root in reality. To begin with they are only half born in Othello. When he is absent from Desdemona the false seeds of fantasy are fed by his fears. When he

is in her presence, however, the truthfulness of her nature breaks
through for him:

> If she be false, O, then heaven mocks itself!
> I'll not believe't.
>
> (*Othello* III 3 275–6)

But more and more he gives in to the infection of doubt. Once
we pass a certain point in our fear and suspicions of another we
are easily persuaded by the most inconclusive of evidences. As
Iago says upon planting one of Desdemona's handkerchiefs in
Cassio's bedchamber,

> ...Trifles light as air
> Are to the jealous confirmations strong
> As proofs of holy writ.
>
> (*Othello* III 3 319–21)

Othello's sleep and tranquillity of mind are now plagued by
unrest. In soliloquy Iago says of him,

> ...Not poppy, nor mandragora,
> Nor all the drowsy syrups of the world,
> Shall ever medicine thee to that sweet sleep
> Which thou owed'st yesterday.
>
> (*Othello* III 3 326–9)

And as Othello himself recognizes,

> ...O, now, for ever
> Farewell the tranquil mind! Farewell content!
>
> (*Othello* III 3 344–5)

To give room to doubt in relationship is to find ourselves haunted
by uncertainties. To open the door to a fear of infidelity is to be
crowded in upon with anxieties that can overwhelm our inner
sight and peace of mind.

For a time the tempest in Othello's mind is a conflict between
doubting and believing. He says to Iago,

> I think my wife be honest, and think she is not;
> I think that thou art just, and think thou art not.
> I'll have some proof.
>
> (*Othello* III 3 381–3)

And yet without any proof, apart from the handkerchief falsely planted in Cassio's bedroom, Othello topples headlong into an abyss of jealousy and rage,

> All my fond love thus do I blow to heaven:
> 'Tis gone.
> Arise, black vengeance, from thy hollow cell!
> Yield up, O love, thy crown and hearted throne
> To tyrannous hate!
>
> (*Othello* III 3 442–6)

Dementing jealousies can erupt almost out of nowhere in our souls, twisting love into fear and affection into anger. The energy that at one point takes the form of tender love can shift at the next into violent hatred. Hurt and rejection, whether real or imagined, ignite feelings of vengeance in us, and in our pain we lash out. Othello and Iago kneel to make a vow to hatred. 'Damn her, lewd minx! O, damn her, damn her!' (*Othello* III 3 472), cries Othello. They begin to plan the death of Desdemona, Iago in his bitter scheming, Othello in his rage of jealousy.

What is it that gives birth to jealousy in the human soul? How does it have such power? When Desdemona begins to sense Othello's jealous spirit, she says to her waiting woman Emilia that she has never given him cause to be suspicious. Emilia responds,

> But jealous souls will not be answered so;
> They are not ever jealous for the cause,
> But jealous for they're jealous. It is a monster
> Begot upon itself, born on itself.
>
> (*Othello* III 4 155–8)

Sometimes the occasion for jealousy is real rather than imagined, but Emilia's words point to the root of jealousy. It is born out of an emptiness in our depths, out of a 'hollow cell' as Othello calls it, that breeds fears and deep uncertainties in us. The jealousy that is conceived in that place cannot be soothed by reason or by the facts of what has or has not happened. It has a life of its own. It is born out of a lack of love for the self. It can be healed only by the recovery of such love.

Othello in his mad rage smothers Desdemona in her bed. Neither knowing nor loving himself, he kills the one who most knows and loves him. As his own soul struggles for breath he suffocates the very one who could have helped him breathe. It is when we are most unsure of our own soul that we attack those who know us best. Uncertain of our own centre we assail those who are our greatest stability.

Immediately the truth of the story unfolds. It becomes clear to Emilia that her husband, Iago, has been responsible for orchestrating the cruel deception and jealousy. When he tries to silence her, she says,

> 'Twill out, 'twill out. I peace?
> No, I will speak as liberal as the north;
> Let heaven, and men, and devils, let them all,
> All, all cry shame against me, yet I'll speak.
>
> (*Othello* V 2 217–20)

She speaks with the force of truth. She expresses the strength of her friendship. Iago says, 'Be wise, and get you home.' But Emilia is undaunted. She responds, 'I will not' (*Othello* V 2 221–2).

Iago's falseness is exposed by Emilia's determination, but the final scene of the play is haunted by a silence as to the why of evil. The penitent and distraught Othello, before taking his own life, asks why Iago 'hath thus ensnared' his soul and body. Iago replies,

> Demand me nothing; what you know, you know:
> From this time forth I never will speak word.
>
> (*Othello* V 2 299–301)

Evil never offers a self-explanation. We may understand some of the contributing factors to deeds of terrible wrong in our lives and world, but always we are left unable to fully comprehend why the human soul descends into such hellishly destructive behaviour. The desire for love and friendship is so deep in the mystery of our being that understanding reaches only so far in explaining its expressions and its perversions. Whether surging from the true heart of our soul or from the depths of the shadow in us, human passion cannot be captured by reason.

The only character in Shakespeare's canon of tragedy who expresses a greater infection of evil than Iago is Aaron the Moor in *Titus Andronicus*. He is responsible for instigating some of the most horrendous inhumanities imaginable. They equal the sort of deep wrongs that we have known in the history of peoples and nations, where evil erupts from deep recesses in the human spirit. In *Titus Andronicus* it is Aaron who engineers the rape of the innocent Lavinia and the cutting off of her hands and tongue so that she cannot communicate who has done the wrong. When finally his evildoings are exposed and he is asked if there is any remorse in him, Aaron responds,

> Ay, that I had not done a thousand more.
> Even now I curse the day, and yet I think
> Few come within the compass of my curse,
> Wherein I did not some notorious ill:
> As kill a man, or else devise his death;
> Ravish a maid, or plot the way to do it;
> Accuse some innocent, and forswear myself;
> Set deadly enmity between two friends;
> Make poor men's cattle break their necks;
> Set fire on barns and haystacks in the night
> And bid the owners quench them with their tears.
> Oft have I digged up dead men from their graves
> And set them upright at their dear friends' doors,
> Even when their sorrows almost were forgot,
> And on their skins, as on the bark of trees,
> Have with my knife carved in Roman letters
> 'Let not your sorrow die, though I am dead.'
> But I have done a thousand dreadful things
> As willingly as one would kill a fly,
> And nothing grieves me heartily indeed
> But that I cannot do ten thousand more.
>
> (*Titus* V 1 124–44)

Aaron embodies a perversion of the deepest energies in the human spirit for love and friendship. He manifests in the extreme the pattern that has been noted in every character of falseness and hatred, the lack of love for others being linked inextricably to a lack of love for the self. As the duchess says in *Richard II*, 'love loving not itself none other can' (*Richard II* V 3 87).

Love Reborn

How do we move in our lives from a lack of love to a recovery of love? How are we to approach that part of us that loves 'not itself' and therefore 'none other can'? As terrifying and intriguing as characters of hatred are, their opposition to love is an expression not of what is true in us but of what is false. They reflect not the heart of our being but a perversion of our human nature. In *Macbeth* the doctor who is tending Lady Macbeth speaks of her sickness as 'unnatural' (*Macbeth* V 1

67). It has resulted from the inhumanities that she and Macbeth have perpetrated. Such wrongdoing is opposed to what is first in us. It conflicts with what is archetypal in the soul. Our healing lies in a return to our true nature.

The Countess Rossillion in *All's Well That Ends Well* says that love and its 'strong passion' is 'the show and seal of nature's truth' (*All's Well* I 3 127). Not only does love 'show' the deepest truth of our nature, it is the 'seal' of what is first in us. The act of loving renews what is at the heart of our being. It seals or confirms in us the pattern of soul that is deeper than the confusions and failures of our relationships.

Many characters in Shakespeare are renewed by the experience of love. In *A Midsummer Night's Dream* the main players in the drama are transformed by what Titania, Queen of the unseen world, calls 'fairy grace' (*Midsummer* V 1 389). It restores them to themselves. It reawakens a naturalness of love in them. Deepest in our nature is the longing to give and receive in relationship. The extent to which we deny these longings is the extent to which we become unnatural.

Among the most delightful of transformations is the 'show and seal' of love that occurs between Beatrice and Benedick in *Much Ado About Nothing*. To begin with they are both firmly closed to love. 'I had rather hear my dog bark at a crow than a man swear he loves me' (*Much Ado* I 1 90), says Beatrice. And as Benedick responds to the notion of relationship with the loquacious Beatrice,

If her breath were as terrible as her terminations,
there were no living near her; she would infect to
the north star. I would not marry her, though she
were endowed with all that Adam had left him before
he transgressed.

(*Much Ado* II 1 227–31)

But when Beatrice is tricked by her friends into believing that Benedick desires her, love begins to work its transformation in her soul. She opens to a world of feeling and desire within herself that formerly she had kept tightly locked, even from her own consciousness. In soliloquy she says,

. . . Benedick, love on; I will requite thee,
Taming my wild heart to thy loving hand.

(*Much Ado* III 1 111–12)

53

Similarly Benedick, led to believe that Beatrice loves him, experiences a sudden conversion within himself. Having so ridiculed love in the past, he argues,

> ... I will be horribly in love with her. I may chance have
> some odd quirks and remnants of wit broken on me,
> because I have railed so long against marriage; but
> doth not the appetite alter? A man loves the meat
> in his youth that he cannot endure in his age. ...
> No, the world must be peopled. When I said I would
> die a bachelor, I did not think I should live till I
> were married.
>
> (*Much Ado* II 3 228–37)

Benedick's attempt to save face is amusing but in the end his experience of love is moving. His newfound desire reconfirms what is deep in the human soul, our longing for relationship.

Benedick and Beatrice, like Romeo and Juliet and all those who are transformed in relationship, discover that it is in giving and receiving that they become truly themselves. They find that their true centre is something that meets and merges with the other. It is not self-contained. They discover also that the love that flows in them is more than an individual possession. To withhold it is opposed to the very nature of love. As Viola says in *Twelfth Night* to the Countess who has closed herself off to the possibility of love, 'what is yours to bestow is not yours to reserve' (*Twelfth Night* I 5 181). It flows in and through us, and we have the power to obstruct it, but it flows for one another.

Love, says one of the lords of Navarre in *Love's Labour's Lost*, is the greatest 'treasure' (*Love's Labour* IV 3 362). It belongs, however, not to any one person, or to only one type of relationship, but to all things. While we may experience it first in relation to one individual, it is given for the well-being of every relationship. It is given that we may become more alive to the whole of life. Love is the grace that awakens us to our full nature,

> It adds a precious seeing to the eye:
> A lover's eyes will gaze an eagle blind.
> A lover's ear will hear the lowest sound ...
> Love's tongue proves dainty Bacchus gross in taste.
>
> (*Love's Labour* IV 3 309–15)

We may see it first in the eyes of a lover, but these, he says,

> ... are the books, the arts, the academes,
> That show, contain, and nourish all the world.
>
> *(Love's Labour* IV 3 328–9)

In love we see the mystery that has given birth to the universe. We glimpse 'the Promethean fire' that blazes from the heart of life.

The giving and receiving of love further opens our souls. And it makes us more alive to the moment, for the time of love is every moment. It is now. It belongs not primarily to the past or the future but to the heart of the present. As Feste the fool sings of love in *Twelfth Night*,

> What is love? 'Tis not hereafter;
> Present mirth hath present laughter,
> What's to come is still unsure.
> In delay there lies no plenty –
> Then come kiss me, sweet and twenty.
>
> *(Twelfth Night* II 3 45–9)

Love is not primarily about wishing that we had loved yesterday or hoping that we will love tomorrow. Love is knowing that we are in relationship now. It is knowing the relationship that is in and between all things, and choosing to give and receive in that relationship. The kissing of someone who is 'sweet and twenty' may awaken us to the 'fire' of life, but love is as much to do with what is not sweet and more than twenty. It is about embracing life from the archetypal depths of the lover and friend in us. It is about being truly alive to relationship whether we like all its details or not.

As the song that ends *Love's Labour's Lost* reminds us, love is not just in the spring,

> When daisies pied and violets blue ...
> Do paint the meadows with delight.
>
> *(Love's Labour* V 2 883–6)

Love is also in the cold and discomfort of winter,

> When icicles hang by the wall ...
> While greasy Joan doth keel the pot ...
> And Marian's nose looks red and raw ...
>
> *(Love's Labour* V 2 901–13)

The time of giving and receiving is now, and without it there would be no now.

III

The Judge and the Warrior

*'Go to your bosom, knock there, and ask your heart
what it doth know.'*
(*Measure for Measure* II 2 136–7)

The True Judge and Warrior

There is a capacity within us to know the truth. The archetypes of judge and warrior relate to this faculty of knowing. The judge in us discerns what is true. The warrior in our depths is prepared to fight for what is true. The correlation between them is like that of eyes and hands. It is the relationship between perceiving, on the one hand, and acting, on the other. Both seek justice. The strength of the one is to see it and name it. The strength of the other is to battle for it and even to die for it.

The reality in our lives and world is that the truth is often complicated. This can have the effect of paralysing our capacity to see and neutering the energies of the fighter in us. We are not quite sure what to think and we do not know how we should act. Truth's complexity can be further exaggerated by those who hold power – politically, scientifically, religiously – in an attempt to disable the critical judgement of those who do not hold power. The suggestion is that only the experts can offer clear judgement, and that it is naive to argue with them. Sometimes this is the case. Usually, however, it is the simplicity of truth that most escapes us. Our lives and our world are filled with situations of injustice that we could unhesitatingly name as wrong and act against. Why do we not?

Some of our separation from the archetypal depths of the judge and warrior in us is self-chosen. Whether it is naming and confronting wrong in our families, on our streets, in our societies or throughout the world, there is cost involved. To resist the flow, to call for change, and to shape our lives according to the perceptions of truth and justice that arise within us is demanding. And so we choose to gag the judge and lock up the warrior. This tendency in us is caricatured by Shakespeare in many of his public-servant characters. In *2 Henry IV* his judges are named 'Shallow' and 'Silence', pointing to our superficiality of judgement and reluctance to speak out against wrong. Correspondingly his soldiers, in their lack of strength and inactivity, are called 'Feeble' and 'Mouldy'.

We may choose, for the sake of short-term comfort, to separate ourselves from the sharp insights and passion of the judge and warrior in us. We cannot, however, cut ourselves off from the repercussions of falsehood and abuse of power. They are all around us and within us in our relationships and experiences of life. As the wrongfully banished duke in *As You Like It* says to another exile in the Forest of Arden,

> Thou seest we are not all alone unhappy.
> This wide and universal theatre
> Presents more woeful pageants than the scene
> Wherein we play in.

> (*As You* II 7 137–40)

The stage of our lives is crowded with wrong. The pain and the struggle that result involve each one of us. Whether we are victim or wrongdoer, or simply onlooker, we are implicated in the drama.

The archetypal energies in us of the judge and warrior carry the force of truth. Both strive to bring light to the complicated and hidden 'pageants' of wrong in our lives. They represent that part of us that believes in openness and in the liberating power of what is true. Queen Katherine, unjustly treated by her husband Henry VIII, warns those who are perverting truth in a complicity of falsehood with the king, 'truth loves open dealing' (*Henry VIII* III 1 39). It seeks the light of day and exposes the concealed compartments of deception and pretence. When we try to cover truth in the relationships of our lives the judge and warrior in us are sapped of their strength. They either fade or take on the distortions of the shadow.

The Judge and Truth

Central to the judge archetype is a sense of truth being greater than us. It is not of our own making and is not to be manipulated. The judge serves truth rather than truth serving the judge. Any attempt at reversing that role creates injustice and in the end will fail. 'Heaven is above all yet,' says Queen Katherine to the twisters of truth in the royal court. 'There sits a judge that no king can corrupt' (*Henry VIII* III 1 100–1). Truth is free. It will not be possessed by us. Ultimately it refuses enslavement. As even the false Claudius recognizes in *Hamlet*, 'in the corrupted currents of this world offence's gilded hand may shove by justice. . . . But 'tis not so above.' In heaven, he says, there is no 'shuffling' of truth (*Hamlet* III 3 58–61). It will not be pushed aside. It cannot be bought out.

In the short term, however, truth is repeatedly sidelined or shoved into submission. It ranks low on our scale of priorities when we would prefer our falseness or our complicity in wrong not to be named by the inner voice of the judge in us. It is muzzled when as societies or nations we embark on a course that violates the life or the sovereignty of another people. We force it into service and justify ourselves by it. Truth is ours we seem to say, with the clear implication that it is not others'.

As ever, Shakespeare's Sir John Falstaff provides us with some of the most candid expressions of our tendency to manage truth for our own advantage. When his friend Prince Hal becomes king, Falstaff assumes that justice will now be at his beck and call. 'The laws of England are at my commandment,' he claims and, with a comic adaptation of the beatitudes, says, 'Blessed are they that have been my friends' (*2 Henry IV* V 3 134–5). And 'woe' to those who have not been his friends.

Although Falstaff's intention represents a manipulation of justice, we laugh because we recognize this tendency in ourselves. It is the pattern of looking after oneself and one's own, as well as exploiting an occasion for getting back at others. A much more sinister misuse of justice occurs in King Lear's family following his resignation from power. Plotting to do wrong for their own ends, they attempt to cover their misdeeds with 'the form of justice'. Lear's son-in-law Cornwall says, 'our power shall do a curtsy to our wrath' (*Lear* III 25–6). It is a pretence at lawfulness. The reality is a monstrous pursuit of power under the guise of legality.

The true judge sees justice as above us. It is not to be coerced into service. One of the shadow tendencies of the judge, however, is to see truth as so much above us that we do not also attend to it within us. We objectify truth and its perversions to the point of distancing them from our own soul. This leads to a type of disengagement in which we feel so removed from acts of wrong that we no longer identify with those who have committed them. We become blind to seeing ourselves in others' transgressions. We fail to recognize in their violations patterns that we too are prone to, and given the same conditions might well capitulate to.

Jaques in his seven ages of man speech in *As You Like It* describes the judge as having a 'fair round belly, with good capon lined' (*As You* II 7 155). The well-fed judge who, as the line suggests, has likely been bribed with food is miles removed from the hunger and want at the back of much crime. It is a picture of the judge cushioned from the real struggles of life. It speaks not only of possible corruption but of a loss of understanding. The shadow in us tries to exercise judgement without empathy. It claims to perceive what is just from the outside without knowing the personal factors from the inside.

Measure for Measure explores this theme in detail. It is the story of Angelo, a lord in Vienna, temporarily deputizing for the absent duke. One of the citizens, Claudio, is charged with fornication for getting his beloved with child outside the bonds of marriage. The letter of the law states that Claudio should die for the offence and Angelo proceeds to enforce it. When Claudio's sister Isabella protests, seeking a degree of mercy and understanding, Angelo responds, 'It is the law, not I, condemns your brother' (*Measure* II 2 80). Even if Claudio were his son, he says, the punishment would need to be executed.

Angelo is a man out of touch with his own humanity and with his own inner longings. He attempts to excuse his merciless stance by appealing to the sanctity of law. The shadow of the judge obscures the ability in him to relate and understand. As the Duke earlier says of Angelo, he 'scarce confesses that his blood flows' (*Measure* I 3 51–2). Or put less delicately by another citizen of Vienna, 'when he makes water his urine is congealed ice' (*Measure* III 2 104–5). Angelo refuses to relate to the predicament of the lovers and the passion for intimacy that has been born between them. He so exalts the law as above us that he neglects to consult his own heart as part of the exercising of true judgement. Isabella pleads with him, 'Go to your bosom, knock there, and ask your heart what it doth know' (*Measure* II 2 136–7). But the shadow that has consumed Angelo is obsessed with legality not with empathy.

Because he is unwilling to consult his heart, this 'well-seeming Angelo' in fact becomes deeply false (*Measure* III 1 224). Although his blood might have seemed 'snow-broth' to begin with (*Measure* I 4 58), he becomes inflamed with desire for Isabella. The very act that he publicly condemns he now, behind closed doors, seeks to force on Claudio's chaste sister, promising that he will reverse his sentence on her brother if she consents to sleep with him. When she threatens to expose him in public, Angelo moves even further into deception and warns her, 'Say what you can, my false o'erweighs your true' (*Measure* II 4 170). The false judge uses outward appearance to cover hidden wrong. He attempts to intimidate the powerless with the strength of public respectability. But his pursuit of truth is at the surface only. A chasm of deceit stretches between the inner and the outer. As the Duke later comments on Angelo, 'what may man within him hide, though angel on the outward side?' (*Measure* III 2 259–60). The shadow forces the judge to live a divided life but in the end the incompatibility is intolerable and the falseness of Angelo is brought to light.

A similar tension between the outer and inner, or between law and spirit, is explored in *The Merchant of Venice*. The merchant Antonio agrees to bail his friend Bassanio out of debt by borrowing funds from the money-lending Shylock. The terms of the contract are strict. It demands full repayment on a particular date. In the event of non-payment, says Shylock to the merchant, 'an equal pound of your fair flesh' is to be cut out (*Merchant* I 3 146–7). The moneylender is determined to abide by the letter of the law. He claims it as absolute.

For Shylock truth, including religious truth, is essentially separate from us. Its root is to be found not in the human heart but beyond us. It demands our obedience in the form of an external law. Those who observe the truth are clean. Those who do not are unclean and there is to be no close intermingling between the two. This is Shylock's perception of Judaism's truth. He uses it to separate himself from others. 'I will buy with you, sell with you', he says to Bassanio, 'but I will not eat with you . . . nor pray with you' (*Merchant* I 3 33–5). Truth is not the common inheritance of humanity. It is the preserve of an elect company.

This approach to truth even leads Shylock to cut off his daughter when she no longer abides by the law. She elopes with a gentile, taking some of Shylock's wealth with her. In response he says, 'I would my daughter were dead at my foot, and the jewels in her ear!' (*Merchant* III 1 83–4). Guided by a law of retribution, he follows not a father's heart but a path that sets the keepers of law irrevocably opposed to the breakers of law. And when the merchant Antonio's argosy is lost at sea, along with the latter's ability to repay the loan, Shylock gloats, 'Good news, good news!' (*Merchant* III 1 99). It is the opposite of good news. Only someone who has denied their own sympathy of heart in favour of devotion to vengeance could regard it as good.

Shylock, however, is not entirely cut off from his heart. We catch a glimpse of it in its woundedness when he alludes to the hurt he has suffered as a Jew at the hands of Christian bigotry,

> Hath not a Jew eyes? Hath not a Jew hands, organs,
> dimensions, senses, affections, passions? – fed with
> the same food, hurt with the same weapons, subject
> to the same diseases, healed by the same means,
> warmed and cooled by the same winter and summer as
> a Christian is? If you prick us, do we not bleed? If you
> tickle us, do we not laugh? If you poison us, do we not die?
>
> (*Merchant* III 1 55–61)

His heart knows the common ground within humanity but his hurt closes him to anything like a genuine openness to those outside his tight boundaries of truth.

We find the same hardening of heart in *Measure for Measure* when Angelo does not allow himself to be touched by human pity and when, as he wrestles with sexual desire, he refuses to relate his own struggle to the experience of the man he has mercilessly sentenced to death. When Angelo begins to try to converse with his own soul and attempts to pray, he finds himself closed off to such depths. 'God in my mouth,' he says, 'as if I did but only chew His name' (*Measure* II 4 4–5). To be cut off from our true depths is to be cut off from truth, just as to reject what is true is to reject the archetypal depths of our own being. It is to separate ourselves from the seeing of the judge within us and to live blindly. As the King of France in *All's Well That Ends Well* says to the young count who has been false in his relationships, if you are 'well acquainted with yourself' you will speak the truth (*All's Well* V 3 106). It is when we do not know our own soul that we are most liable to distort the truth. It is when we invest more heavily in outward appearance than in inner reality that we are most likely to be false. In *Cymbeline* the repentant prince vows to reverse the fashion of the world. 'Less without and more within', he says (*Cymbeline* V 1 33). Less regard to outward standards of correctness and more attention to the motions of the heart is what will awaken the archetypal strengths of the judge in us.

But how do we learn to consult the inner text of truth as well as weighing up outward evidence? How do we withstand the mighty pressure of external standards and majority opinion, neither of which may be true? As the prologue to *2 King Henry IV* asks, 'which of you will stop the vent of hearing when loud Rumour speaks ... stuffing the ears of men with false reports?' (*2 Henry IV* Induction 1–8). The answer does not lie in refusing to listen to others or in dismissing out of hand the patterns of insight that have come down to us in our respective traditions. The answer is more to do with how we listen and how we encounter the assumptions of our communities.

In *Much Ado About Nothing* the bride Hero is wrongly accused of faithlessness. Even her betrothed believes the false reports. To begin with her father too is swayed by the apparent evidence. In time, however, he begins to listen within himself to a deep certainty of his daughter's innocence. 'My soul doth tell me Hero is belied', he says (*Much Ado* V 1 42). Our inner perceptions can of course be confused. We will sometimes see only what we want to see. Our inner sight will not improve, however, if we do not use it. We will not come to trust its wisdom unless we test it.

Within the archetypal depths of the human mystery is a faculty of knowing that is deeper than external appearances. The discerning eye of the judge is part of our nature. It views falseness and wrongdoing as essentially unnatural. It affirms goodness and truth as an expression of health and of our true nature. In the tragedy of Hamlet when the ghost of the murdered king reveals the 'horrible' deed of his murder, he says to *Hamlet*, 'if thou hast nature in thee, bear it not' (*Hamlet* I 5 81). The judge in our depths is repelled by wrong and instinctively wants to name it. Hidden falseness is intolerable and needs to be laid bare. It is this that fuels Hamlet's fury and inspires his determination to expose the murderer.

When the true judge in us is fully awakened to the monstrosity of cruel deeds it wakes with a passion of strength for it issues from a place deep within us. Hamlet confronts his mother with the truth of the murder and names her own betrayal of the memory of his father. 'Speak to me no more', she says. 'These words like daggers enter in mine ears' (*Hamlet* III 4 95–6). The speaking of truth has a power to it. It can pierce the false heart and open it to change. It wounds in order to heal. As Hamlet later comments on his actions, 'I must be cruel only to be kind' (*Hamlet* III 4 179). Or as the speaker of truth says in *The Winter's Tale*, true words are like a medicine prescribed by a 'physician' (*Winter* II 3 54). It may be hard to administer, but a belief in the healing power of truth emboldens the judge to speak.

The Judge and Grace

But the speaking of truth is not enough in and by itself, nor is the exercising of justice in all its force. The true word needs to be received if it is to work its healing power. The perpetrators of wrong need more than retribution on its own to experience a change of heart. There are limits to what justice can do within us and between us, no matter how powerfully applied. As Isabella in *Measure for Measure* says to Angelo in relation to his strict enforcement of the law, ''tis excellent to have a giant's strength, but it is tyrannous to use it like a giant' (*Measure* II 2 107–9). The punishing application of force does not engender repentance, nor does it give birth to a genuine desire for new directions. The restraining power of force is required if justice is to be implemented, but to depend entirely on force is the giant's way not the human way. It makes 'the angels weep', says Isabella (*Measure* II 2 122). It is a violation of human authority.

So what else does the judge require besides force? Even before Angelo as judge becomes false in his manipulation of power, his execution of justice is inadequate because it lacks understanding and a willingness to be merciful. Isabella asks him, 'How would you be, if He, which is the top of judgement, should but judge you as you are?' (*Measure* II 2 75–7). How would any of us fair in the important relationships of our lives and world if we were dealt with merely in terms of justice? The policy of measure for measure, or an eye for an eye, plays a part in the just governing of society and human relationship but it is only a part. As Mahatma Gandhi the great seeker of justice in twentieth-century India contended, if we were to live only by the principle of an eye for an eye, in the end the whole world would be blind.

Without mercy no relationship can stand. In *Measure for Measure* Angelo learns this the hard way. His falseness is exposed and he sees clearly that if he is to be judged as he has judged then he will die. Without mercy there is no hope. Or as Angelo says, 'when once our grace we have forgot, nothing goes right' (*Measure* IV 4 31–2). No dimension of human life, which is a web of interdependent relationships, can survive without the flow of grace. If the judge in us depends only on justice then we will destroy one another with the sword of truth.

In *The Merchant of Venice* the money-lender Shylock forgets grace and in the end nothing goes right for him. When Antonio is arrested for lack of repayment, Shylock says, 'Tell not me of mercy' (*Merchant* III 3 1). He refuses to allow grace to be part of his decision. So obsessed is he with his right of retribution that he will not listen to Antonio's pleas,

> I'll have my bond. I will not hear thee speak.
> I'll have my bond; and therefore speak no more.
> I'll not be made a soft and dull-eyed fool,
> To shake the head, relent, and sigh, and yield
> To Christian intercessors. ...
> I'll have no speaking; I will have my bond.
>
> (*Merchant* III 3 12–17)

Shylock's insistence that he will not hear Antonio speak is a major feature of justice closing itself to mercy. When the judge in us chooses to be deaf to the voice of another we have decided to distance ourselves from grace.

At Antonio's trial in Venice his friend Bassanio offers to double the repayment in order to secure Antonio's release, to which Shylock replies that he would reject even twelve times the total. Antonio has failed to repay the loan and Shylock seeks nothing but the terms of the contract, a pound of Antonio's flesh. When he is asked how he would ever hope to find mercy himself, in that he offers none, Shylock responds, 'What judgment shall I dread, doing no wrong?' (*Merchant* IV 1 89). It is the voice of justice cut off from the giving and receiving of grace. It is the blind judge in us not recognizing our own need for mercy. Shylock demands that the letter of the law be fulfilled,

> The pound of flesh which I demand of him,
> Is dearly bought, is mine, and I will have it.
> If you deny me, fie upon your law!
> There is no force in the decrees of Venice.
> I stand for judgment. Answer; shall I have it?
>
> (*Merchant* IV 1 100–4)

When it looks as if there can be no answer in law but the granting of Shylock's demand, he begins to sharpen his knife on the sole of his boots in readiness to cut out the pound of flesh that he is owed. Antonio's friend Gratiano observes to Shylock, 'Not on thy sole, but on thy soul . . . thou mak'st thy knife keen' (*Merchant* IV 1 123–4). Shylock's heart has become as hard as flint. The refusal to consult mercy has made his soul like stone. 'Can no prayers pierce thee?', asks Gratiano (*Merchant* IV 1 126). Shylock's response conveys the inflexibility of judgement when it is untempered by grace: 'I stand here for law', he says (*Merchant* IV 1 142). If judgement is uninformed by mercy then its enforcement carries a black and white simplicity. There is no choice but to follow the law.

But the course of justice in *The Merchant of Venice* takes a new direction with the appearance of the young Portia disguised as a doctor of law. She can be seen as the feminine within the judge. She carries the softening powers of grace into the hard realm of justice. She represents a holding together of heart and head, of feeling and reason. But she does not do it in a way that sacrifices justice. Although she knows its limitations she also knows that it must not be disregarded. 'In the course of justice, none of us should see salvation', she says (*Merchant* IV 1 201–2). But when one of Antonio's friends suggests that she therefore bend the law, Portia is firm in her response. 'To do a great right, do a little wrong', Bassanio had advised her, 'and curb this cruel devil of his will.'

Portia's reply is, 'It must not be. ... It cannot be' (*Merchant* IV 1 215–20). She is guided by grace but the true judge in her will not disregard the law.

So what is the place of justice in its full force if we are to be guided above all else by grace? Part of what is being pointed to is the power of truth and the importance of the judge unequivocally naming wrong when it occurs. Nothing can replace the bringing of truth into the light. 'Truth loves open dealing', as we have heard Queen Katherine say. The movement of grace happens not in opposition to a clear exposing of falsehood or a fierce protection of the law. It happens rather in and through the denouncing of wrong and the pronouncing of what is right. Grace is given not to impede the pursuit of justice. It is given to move beyond it, for grace believes not only in the force of truth but in the power of mercy.

In *The Merchant of Venice* the wise Portia uses grace not to skirt around truth or to pervert the course of justice but to move through it to a deeper place, the opportunity for mercy. Antonio has been unable to repay the loan according to the terms of the contract. To that extent Shylock is justified in his claims. Portia therefore concludes that he is to have his pound of flesh. She also declares, however, that he is not to take a fraction more or a fraction less and that he must not spill any blood. The bond entitles him only to a pound of flesh. Anything else and he will have broken the law. Furthermore, the statutes of Venice protect its citizens from attempts on their life and it is clear that Shylock has been contriving to take the life of Antonio. Portia therefore declares him guilty of a major offence. His life now lies at the mercy of the Duke of Venice, who in the end pardons him. 'When mercy seasons justice', says Portia, we are most like God (*Merchant* IV 1 199). The naming of truth and the denouncing of wrong take us only so far. The exercising of mercy can take us further. 'It is twice blest', she says. 'It blesseth him that gives and him that takes' (*Merchant* IV 1 185–6). It frees the giver from bitterness, and in the taker it releases new beginnings.

The Passion of the Warrior

Whereas the judge in us sees wrong and names it, with the possibility also of exercising mercy, the archetypal energy of the warrior in us flows towards fighting wrong and defeating it. The warrior too can be guided by mercy. But again mercy does not impede the path of pursuing justice. It does not suppress the desire in us to fight wrong, just as it does not eclipse our faculty for naming wrong. Rather it frees the warrior to move beyond the goal of simply defeating the enemy.

In *Antony and Cleopatra*, the Queen of Egypt refers to her lover as 'the greatest soldier of the world' (*Antony* I 3 38). By the time we get to know him in the play, however, the sharpness of the warrior in Antony has been dulled. The lover's shadow has been cast over him. His warring strength has been sapped, 'my sword made weak by my affection', as he later recognizes (*Antony* III 11 67). But we see the continuing marks of the warrior in some of Antony's men. Enobarbus, for instance, speaks his mind at a meeting of political leaders. When Antony, having already lost much of the soldier's forthrightness of speech, reprimands Enobarbus, the latter responds, 'that truth should be silent I had almost forgot'. Antony replies, 'speak no more' (*Antony* II 2 112–13). It is an attempt to dampen the directness of the warrior. Enobarbus does not mince his words. The warrior is intolerant of duplicity and lack of candour.

We see this in the great Roman soldier Coriolanus. As one of his friends says of him, 'He would not flatter Neptune for his trident. . . . His heart's his mouth' (*Coriolanus* III 1 255–6). He says what he feels and does not tailor his statements to curry favour. His approach to the crowds is 'neither to care whether they love or hate him' (*Coriolanus* II 2 11–12). The warrior in us utters from our conviction of what is right and not from our perception of what others want to hear. It is that part of us that remains undistracted by whether or not we are liked.

In *King Lear*, a story of conflict between good and evil, there is a major distinction between the true warrior and the false warrior. Edgar, the faithful son of Gloucester who defends the wronged king, says, 'Speak what we feel, not what we ought to say' (*Lear* V 3 322). On the other hand Edmund his brother, who lies to his father and plots against Lear, calls this 'foolish honesty' (*Lear* I 2 177). He regards it as an unwise tactic. The difference is a confidence in truth, based also on a relationship to truth. The archetype of the warrior is wedded to what is right, not only as the goal of fighting but as the means to that end.

This can lead to the caricature of the warrior as someone who fights over almost everything nearly all the time. Jaques in his seven ages of man speech describes the soldier as 'sudden and quick in quarrel' (*As You* II 7 152). The impression is of a bad-tempered insecurity, always on the verge of conflict. The true warrior in us, however, knows that in fighting for truth there are times of engagement and times of withdrawal. There are seasons for expending energy and seasons for preserving strength. There is a discerning of which battles to fight and when not to waste one's energy. In the Hebrew scriptures Ecclesiastes says that there is 'a time to take life and a time to heal life . . . a time to tear down and a time to build up . . . a time to embrace and a time to refrain from embracing . . . a time to keep silence and a time to speak . . . a time for war and a time for peace' (Ecclesiastes 3.1–8). The warrior in us knows this. The challenge is to discern what time it is, whether it is the time for war or the time for peace, and in the time of battle to know how to wage war in ways that will allow us to wage peace when the time changes, or in the time of peace to know how to maintain peace in ways that will allow us to fight with all our strength when the time for battle comes.

One of Shakespeare's great warrior figures, King Henry V, advises his soldiers:

> In peace there's nothing so becomes a man
> As modest stillness and humility:
> But when the blast of war blows in our ears,
> Then imitate the action of the tiger;
> Stiffen the sinews, summon up the blood,
> Disguise fair nature with hard-favoured rage;
> Then lend the eye a terrible aspect.
>
> (*Henry V* III 1 3–9)

The warrior is not always in the mode of the fierce tiger. There are the resting times when that dimension of our being is still and even gentle. But do we know the 'terrible aspect' of the warrior in us, that part of our soul that rages at wrong and shakes with anger at lies? If we are out of touch with these depths, or live primarily in fear of them rather than in awe of the strength that is within us, then we are living a type of diminished existence. We have shut down to part of our soul. We are denying a vital dimension of the human mystery.

When the warrior in us awakes to confront wrong, there is no shying away from action. When the time is right the warrior strikes. This is part of the strength of our warring archetype, to deal swiftly and directly with the enemy. In *2 King Henry VI* Richard Plantagenet, having just fought and slain another in battle, says, 'priests pray for enemies, but princes kill' (*2 Henry VI* V 2 71). The enemy does not always have to be killed. This is the prejudice of the shadow warrior – that there is no other way of dealing with one's opponents but to destroy them. The truth of

Plantagenet's utterance, however, is that, while the priest within us will reflect and pray in the face of wrong, the warrior in us wants to respond and act. These are two dimensions of the human soul. We have a capacity for reflection and a capacity for action. It is important to know that both of these energies are part of our archetypal depths. We carry within ourselves the wisdom of the priest and the strength of the warrior. In the midst of conflict we can choose to draw on either or on both.

In *1 Henry IV* the warrior Hotspur, as his name suggests, is quick to act but slow to reflect. Always he is rearing to go and impatient of delay. His directness of speech, 'tell truth and shame the devil' as he says, is equalled by his immediacy of response and the overwhelming desire in him for active engagement (*1 Henry IV* III 1 55). But Hotspur is restless in his obsession with combat. He lives out of only one archetype within himself, and even then out of only one dimension of the warrior, namely the warrior's commitment to action. This compulsion in Hotspur is caricatured in the description of him as one who kills 'some six or seven dozen Scots at a breakfast, washes his hands, and says to his wife "Fie upon this quiet life! I want work"' (*1 Henry IV* II 4 100–3). His appetite for battling is insatiable.

Hotspur gets stuck in one mode of the warrior archetype. He represents that part of us that becomes locked into conflict. It may be an honourable cause but fighting is only ever one way of dealing with a struggle. Hotspur is unaware of other forms of resolving disagreement. Even as lover and friend he disparages what is not related to combative energy. When his wife tries to engage him playfully and lovingly, Hotspur sees it as a distraction from the real focus of life, which is battling for what he believes in. 'This is no world to play', he says 'and to tilt with lips. We must have bloody noses, and cracked crowns' (*1 Henry IV* II 3 94–6). Everything else is subordinated to the fire of the warrior. Dangerously he lives out of only one part of his soul.

The Mercy of the Warrior

For the true warrior 'bloody noses' and 'cracked crowns' are but one feature of fighting for truth. In *Macbeth* when the exiled Scottish thane Macduff receives word that his wife and children have been savagely slaughtered at the command of the tyrant king of Scotland, he is counselled by another lord to 'dispute it like a man'. Macduff responds, 'I shall do so; but I must also feel it like a man' (*Macbeth* IV 3 219–20). Part of the true depth of the warrior in us is to allow ourselves to feel the pain of wrongs, not simply those that touch our lives directly but the injustices that other families and other nations suffer. To be in touch with our emotions is to be more truly alive. It is to open a faculty of knowing in us deeper than reason, and to allow our thinking and our acting to be informed by our feelings.

The Roman general Titus Andronicus, whose entire family is subjected to the terror of rape and violence, grieves the inhumanities that he and others have borne. 'When heaven doth weep', he cries, 'doth not the earth o'erflow?' (*Titus* III 1 221). When what is absolute is violated, should a torrent of feeling not open in us? The passion of the true warrior is inflamed when the sacredness of life is needlessly violated. It is these feelings that fuel the fierce determination to fight wrong. Without them the warrior is only half awake.

To be in touch with our emotions is also to allow the warrior in our depths to be challenged by sympathetic feelings and to be moved by the possibility of mercy. The false Edmund in *King Lear* instructs one of his soldiers to murder the captured king and his faithful daughter Cordelia. Sensing that the soldier might take pity on them, Edmund counsels him to remain hardened in his purpose. 'To be tender-minded,' he says, 'does not become a sword' (*Lear* V 3 32–3). To be open to the genuine movements of the heart is a threat to the shadow warrior. It exposes us to the light of human compassion and the natural desire for relationship.

We see this at work in the encounter between the soldier Hubert and the young Prince Arthur in *King John*. Hubert's mission is to be rid of the boy, who is a claimant to the throne and a threat to the insecure king. As he approaches the deed, however, Hubert says to himself, 'If I talk to him . . . he will awake my mercy, which lies dead. Therefore I will be sudden' (*John* IV 1 25–7). But the soldier is not sudden enough. The boy speaks to him and Hubert's humanity of feeling is reawakened. 'His words do take possession of my bosom', he says (*John* IV 1 32). A sense of relationship with the boy releases him from the shadow warrior. He relents and the true face of his soul re-emerges. As the young prince comments, 'O, now you look like Hubert. All this while you were disguised' (*John* IV 1 125–6). The shadow distorts our countenance. It covers the true self.

Coriolanus, as we have seen, is a great soldier in his bravery and determination. The realm of feelings, however, is one of uncertainty for him, especially when his fighting energies conflict with his family affections. Standing on the outskirts of Rome, which he is planning to attack, he watches his wife, his mother and his young son approach him from the city. They are coming to beg that he reverse his plans, even though he has been unjustly wronged by the Roman people and its leadership. Coriolanus recognizes the force of feeling that now begins to stir in him. Initially his response is, 'I'll never be such a gosling to obey instinct, but stand as if a man were author of himself and knew no other kin' (*Coriolanus* V 3 34–7). The shadow in him wants to isolate the warrior from the husband and the son within himself. It wants to pretend that military action can be taken with no regard to family life, and that a true warrior can ignore the deep natural instincts for relationship that stir within us.

Coriolanus wrestles with his feelings. He does not want to hear his mother name the truth of what is happening in his heart. 'Tell me not wherein I seem unnatural', he says (*Coriolanus* V 3 83–4). But the strength of emotion in him is such that he knows what he must do. He realizes that it would be wrong to ignore his innate sense of family and home, and so he reverses his decision. He also knows, however, that what his emotions have guided him to is perilous in military terms. As he says to his mother, 'most dangerously you have ... prevailed' (*Coriolanus* V 3 188). The shadow warrior likes to pretend that there are neat categories to life and that they do not overlap – the public and the private, them and us, strategy and feeling. The true warrior, on the other hand, knows that the whole of life is interrelated, that acts of war and individual relationship affect each other, and that on both sides of any conflict there is family affection and love that will be touched and torn by war. In the case of Coriolanus there is the recognition that it will be costly for him to integrate the military and the personal.

The shadow of the warrior is powerful in those around Coriolanus. His military colleagues now ridicule him,

> At a few drops of women's rheum, which are
> As cheap as lies, he sold the blood and labour
> Of our great action.
>
> (*Coriolanus* V 6 46–8)

They accuse him of abandoning their victory in favour of affection for his wife and mother. 'Pages blushed at him', says one of the generals, 'and men of heart look'd wondering each at other' (*Coriolanus* V 6 99–100). He is a disgrace because, instead of pursuing the narrow path of what is expected of him by his army, he follows his heart's inclinations. 'Therefore shall he die', says one of the leaders (*Coriolanus* V 6 48). To demand that his soldiers who are fixed on conflict and victory be guided now by compassion is intolerable. They turn on him and a mob tears him to pieces.

The integration of the heart and the head is demanding for the warrior. To be attentive to feelings and to conscience as well as to the mind and to traditional expectations of warring is painful in practice. Again and again there is pressure to let go of the tension and to follow the stereotype of the warrior as one whose determined resolve is beyond the affections of the heart. In *Pericles* the wicked Dionyza instructs her footman to act without compunction in the murder of the innocent princess: 'Let not conscience inflame too nicely; nor let pity... melt thee, but be a soldier to thy purpose' (*Pericles* IV 1 4–8). The impression she creates, and the argument often used in making the case for war, is that it is disloyal or cowardly to be swayed by conscience. The expectation is that the warrior will obey orders and will do so without consulting the heart.

In *King Richard III*, when murderers who have been hired to kill the guiltless Clarence are briefly attentive to their inner sense of what is right and wrong, they note that there are still 'some certain dregs of conscience' in their hearts (*Richard III* I 4 122). They also observe, however, that when the purse of payment is opened 'conscience flies out'. Money dulls their inner sensitivities. As one of them proceeds to say concerning conscience,

> I'll not meddle with it; it makes a man a coward. A man
> cannot steal, but it accuseth him; a man cannot swear,
> but it checks him; a man cannot lie with his neighbour's
> wife, but it detects him. 'Tis a blushing shamefast spirit
> that mutinies in a man's bosom. It fills a man full of
> obstacles. It made me once restore a purse of gold
> that by chance I found. It beggars any man that keeps
> it. It is turned out of towns and cities for a dangerous
> thing, and every man that means to live well endeavours
> to trust to himself and to live without it.
>
> (*Richard III* I 4 135–46)

The soldier is not alone in thinking that it might be easier to live without conscience. It raises the awkward question. It casts doubt on our motives and, in relation to the warrior in us, it constantly asks whether it is right to use force.

This is not to say that there are not occasions when it is right to fight fiercely and to do so with all our strength. It is simply to say that in the heart of the true warrior there will be an attentiveness also to the questions that conscience throws up. The heart will ask if it is right to enter conflict. It will question the use of violence and query the cost to human life. Like Prince Hamlet who witnesses an army marching towards battle to fight for territory that is of little significance, instinctively the heart knows the folly of such enterprise, the 'exposing what is mortal', as Hamlet says, 'even for an eggshell' (*Hamlet* IV 4 51–3). Yet Hamlet is not unaware of the fierce energies of the fighter within himself. When Laertes assaults him at the grave of Ophelia, Hamlet responds,

> I prithee take thy fingers from my throat.
> For, though I am not splenitive and rash,
> Yet have I something in me dangerous,
> Which let thy wisdom fear. Hold off thy hand.
>
> (*Hamlet* V 1 256–9)

Do we know that dimension within us that is 'dangerous', that part of our soul that will not tolerate wrong and that is impatient of abuse? It is the energy that surges up from our depths to defend life and to protect what is sacred. But precisely because it is a dangerous energy it is easily twisted by the shadow into a violence against life and against what is sacred.

To be aware of the archetypal energies of the warrior in us is not always to give way to them, nor is it always to display them like a swaggering soldier. As the great warrior King Henry V says, it is an 'empty vessel' that makes the loudest noise (*Henry V* IV 4 68). To be sounding forth continually with battling bravado speaks more of deep uncertainty than of inner strength. Yet there is the time and the occasion for a fierce showing of the warrior and of bravery. As is said of Coriolanus, once his ire is raised he 'does forget that ever he heard the name of death' (*Coriolanus* III 1 258–9). It is that part of us that is fearless in facing wrong. Without it we live in dread of the enemy, imprisoned by our own hesitations and fears. With it we are emboldened to name and confront the falsenesses that are within us and between us.

Where does our reluctance to be true to the warrior come from? As is often the case, Sir John Falstaff, in whom the shadow is comically to the fore, provides us with expressions of our lack of strength and cowardice. He embodies the belief that life is gained more by protecting ourselves and by taking what circumstances have to offer than by a giving of ourselves and by a releasing of our deepest energies. Reluctantly Falstaff enters battle, and is more concerned about escaping harm than confronting the enemy: 'God keep lead out of me,' he says, 'I need no more weight than my own bowels' (*1 Henry IV* V 3 34–5). And having survived the conflict, mainly by making himself scarce on the battlefield, he concludes by saying, 'The better part of valour is discretion, in the which better part I have saved my life' (*1 Henry IV* V 4 118–20). But what has he saved? He is physically safe, and in that sense has preserved his life. But he is not alive to the passionate depths of the warrior in himself. Neither is he awake to the archetypal longings in the human soul to take risks for what is just and true. He represents a diminution of being alive. His true depths are smothered.

To be in touch with the warrior in ourselves is not to treat war lightly, nor is it to pretend that fighting can achieve everything. In fact the true warrior is appalled by the destruction that war wreaks. It destroys life. It does 'mangle the work of nature', says the King of France. It defaces the 'patterns' of God (*Henry V* II 4 60–1). Sometimes it is necessary, but the warrior's strength, while it can defend what is just and attack what is wrong, in fact has no power to transform the heart of the enemy. The use of force is powerless in the world of the soul.

In *The Two Gentlemen of Verona* one of the so-called 'gentlemen' tries to force a young woman to love him. 'I'll woo you like a soldier', he says (*Gentlemen* V 4 57). His attempts to court her favour have failed, so he threatens to make her love him by physically dominating her, even though, as he himself admits, to do so is 'against the nature of love'. It is as little in the power of a soldier to force a woman's affections as it is in the act of war to make an enemy become a friend. Something much greater than physical force is required.

As with the judge the greatest strength within the warrior is the capacity to be merciful. This is not instead of force. It is, however, greater than force. Only compassion and mercy can create the soil in which reconciliation grows. War cannot do that on its own. It cannot command a change of heart in one's opponent. In *Cymbeline* when the wronged prince, Posthumus, confronts his personal enemy after battle and the latter seeks mercy from him, Posthumus' response is, 'The pow'r that I have on you is to spare you . . . to forgive you. Live,' he says, 'and deal with others better' (*Cymbeline* V 5 421–2). Pardon paves the way for new beginnings. It is the power that allows for the re-creation of relationship. Without it the only possibility is the end of relationship. Cymbeline, the king, calls it 'freeness' (*Cymbeline* V 5 424). It sets the defeated enemy free but it also liberates the warrior to be more than simply a conqueror. To release the flow of mercy in our archetypal depths is to be set free to do something greater even than confronting and defeating wrong. It allows us to be part of the transformation of life.

IV

The Seer and the Mage

*'There are more things in heaven and earth...
than are dreamt of in your philosophy.'*
(*Hamlet* I 5 166–7)

The True Seer and Mage

There are wise women and men in our lives whose wisdom is derived not so much from outward knowledge and learning as from inner perception and intuition. They are aware of the mystery and wonder of life, as they are of its pain and brokenness. Some of the insight that they share at critical moments comes unexpectedly like the presence of wise figures in fairy tales – a grandmother in the forgotten attic of a castle suddenly appearing to comfort the young terrified princess, or a wizened old fairy in the remotest part of a neglected wood meeting the lost prince and in casual conversation dropping the vital clue for his well-being. Wisdom is close to us although we may fail to recognize it. It is within us, waiting to be awakened, even though we may be unaware of its presence. The archetypes of the seer and the mage relate to this inner wisdom.

In *Hamlet* the prince says to his friend,

> There are more things in heaven and earth . . .
> Than are dreamt of in your philosophy.
>
> (*Hamlet* I 5 166–7)

There are heights and depths in life, there are energies within us and around us, that neither physical sight nor sophisticated reason can comprehend. The seer represents that part of us that is alive to the unknown and senses what cannot be captured by outward sight. It is the faculty of knowing associated with what Shakespeare calls our 'inward soul' (*Richard II* II 2 11), the intuitive ability in us to perceive at levels deeper than intellectual formulation.

Similarly the mage, a name that simply means 'the wise one' and shares a common derivation with the word 'magi', is alert to the relationship between the seen and the unseen. The mage follows the signs of heaven on earth, the interweavings of the physical and the spiritual. It is that part of us that is attentive to the interplay of worlds and the concourse between the conscious and the unconscious. Through the perceptions and disciplines of inner sight the mage seeks to transform what is broken and torn in life. The archetype of the mage in us is a healing and restorative presence.

Always what cannot be seen and known outwardly is greater than what can be viewed physically and grasped mentally. Volumnia says to her son in *Coriolanus*, there are 'those mysteries which heaven will not have earth to know' (*Coriolanus* IV 2 35–6). Always there is more mystery in life than understanding. Always the realm of the unconscious far exceeds the field of the conscious. But there is much that we can know. The unseen universe corresponds to the infinity of the physical universe. Although it remains hidden from outward sight there is no end to what can be explored and translated into awareness.

In *Troilus and Cressida* one of the young princes of Troy responds to the leaders of the Greek army who view him limitedly in outward terms,

> O, like a book of sport thou'lt read me o'er;
> But there's more in me than thou understand'st.

> (*Troilus* IV 5 239–40)

The seer and the mage read more deeply than life's surface. They know that in every person and in every created thing there is more than we can ever outwardly understand. They represent archetypal depths of wisdom in us that perceive with inner sight and with an intuition of soul.

These archetypal depths are within each of us although they are more pronounced in certain people than in others, and are clearer at particular moments in our lives than at other moments. The reality is that sometimes our perceptions of the unseen are horribly confused. There is the lunatic, as Theseus says in *A Midsummer Night's Dream*, who 'sees more devils than vast hell can hold' (*Midsummer* V 1 9). The mind of the lunatic is flooded by dementing forces of the unconscious, sometimes precisely because his inner sight is so sensitive. It is not that the inner perceptions of the person suffering from madness have failed entirely, or that everything inwardly seen is unreal. Madness is a continuum on which we all stand. Many of the anxieties and insecurities of our lives are caused by unknown energies that disturb our inner balance. The person who is mentally ill is being overwhelmed by forces which, to varying degrees, are at work in us all.

Then there is the lover, says Theseus, who sees 'more than cool reason ever comprehends' (*Midsummer* V 1 6). The intellect alone cannot perceive the beauty that is in another's eyes or read the passion in one's own heart. Yes, the lover like the lunatic may end up exaggerating what is seen, inflating the attractiveness of the other or the terror of a situation, but in both cases an inner faculty of perception is being exercised that is distinct from outward sight and formal reason. The archetypal vision of the seer is constantly at work in the depths of the human soul and in the interminglings of relationship.

And finally, says Theseus, there is the poet who,

> Doth glance from heaven to earth, from earth to heaven,
> And as imagination bodies forth
> The forms of things unknown, the poet's pen
> Turns them to shapes, and gives to airy nothing
> A local habitation and a name.
>
> (*Midsummer* V 1 13–17)

In the poet the worlds of the unseen and the seen conjoin to conceive of new form and new vitality. This is the creativity of the seer in us – to use our inner perceptions of the unknown to give birth to awarenesses that have never been before and to be part of fresh beginnings in our lives and world that come forth from the invisible into the visible and from the unconscious into the conscious.

Because of the interminglings of the visible and the invisible, it is not away from earth that we are to look for the graces of heaven. The mage searches in and through the elements of creation for heaven's healing gifts. As Helena, the mage-like figure in *All's Well That Ends Well*, says,

> Our remedies oft in ourselves do lie,
> Which we ascribe to heaven.
>
> (*All's Well* I 1 212–13)

She knows that unseen energies for good are coursing through us. She also knows that within us are the darknesses of hell, the destructive inner forces that can tear apart our lives and relationships.

The tension between these energies, and between believing and doubting, is explored in a dialogue between the young Helena and the old King of France who is suffering from what is thought to be an incurable disease. It is the tension that we know in the inner kingdom of our own lives when we are not well within ourselves and fail to recognize the sources of healing that are close at hand, present even in the palace of our own being. Helena, who possesses a knowledge of the healing powers of plants, offers to help the king. The sovereign head of the realm, however, has already been persuaded by his 'learned doctors' that he is beyond help. He regards her hopefulness as 'credulous'. She holds no official status at court and her wisdom has been dismissed by the royal counsellors. Nevertheless, Helena perseveres. 'Of heaven, not me, make an experiment', she says. 'My art is not past power, nor you past cure' (*All's Well* II 1 154–8).

What is it in us or in our relationships that is unwell, so much so that we may have ceased to believe that we can be healed? What have we given up hope about in our lives or world? The mage in us is a healing presence. It is that part of us that accesses hidden sources of well-being. It is also that part of us that continues to hope. 'What I can do can do no hurt to try', says Helena (*All's Well* II 1 134). How open are we to the mage in our own depths? How ready are we to believe that we or others are not 'past cure'?

The mage looks to nature for healing graces, both to the inner nature of humanity and to the physical nature of the created order. He notes, for instance, the naturally restoring powers of rest and sleep. He observes how creation is renewed by its long periods of stillness, the silence of the night giving way to the creative activity of the day, or the quiet winter earth followed by the budding energy of spring. The doctor in *King Lear*, who is summoned to treat the madness of the rejected king, says, 'our foster-nurse of nature is repose' (*Lear* IV 4 12). Rest will restore the king to himself. It is sleep that heals our tired minds and exhausted bodies. Nature, though wounded, carries within itself restorative medicines for our well-being.

The doctor in *The Two Noble Kinsmen* also is a believer in the transforming graces of nature. In particular he prescribes the healing powers of love. On learning that a mentally distracted young woman has sought the affection of her betrothed and that in response he kissed her, the doctor says,

> 'Twas well done; twenty times had been far better,
> For there the cure lies mainly.
>
> (*Kinsmen* V 2 7–8)

Within our natural longings for affection and physical intimacy lie restorative energies for the healing of our minds and souls. As the doctor proceeds to say,

> Lie with her if she asks you . . .
> Please her appetite,
> And do it home; it cures her *ipso facto*.
>
> (*Kinsmen* V 2 17–35)

Not surprisingly the betrothed replies, 'I am of your mind, doctor' (*Kinsmen* V 2 37). Our bodies and souls can know instinctively what is good for them, and part of the healing grace that we carry within ourselves is the deep pleasure that comes with doing what is life-giving.

The mage studies nature. He observes its characteristics and notes the hidden energies that can be found in creation's outward forms and rhythms. Learning, therefore, is respected by the mage, for as Lord Say says in *2 King Henry VI*,

> ... ignorance is the curse of God,
> Knowledge the wing wherewith we fly to heaven.
>
> (*2 Henry VI* IV 7 68–9)

Learning provides tools of awareness that can help us be attentive to the convergence of the seen and the unseen and to the healing properties that lie within the physical.

In *2 King Henry VI* we also find the anti-type of the mage in the character of Jack Cade, an anarchist insurrectionist who recognizes only what outwardly can be seen and handled and who suspects all learning. Accusing Lord Say of being a traitor to the people, he says,

> ... It will be proved to thy face that thou hast men
> about thee that usually talk of a noun and a verb,
> and such abominable words as no Christian ear
> can endure to hear.
>
> (*2 Henry VI* IV 7 34–7)

Instead of reverencing knowledge he fears it. Instead of allowing learning to further open him to the interwovenness of life he shuts down to anything that is unknown to him. Concerning the educated Lord Say, he concludes, 'Away with him! Away with him! He speaks Latin' (*2 Henry VI* IV 7 53).

But the knowledge of the mage is not simply a head knowledge. It is the type of knowing expressed by the banished Duke in *As You Like It* which,

> Finds tongues in trees, books in the running brooks,
> Sermons in stones, and good in every thing.
>
> (*As You* II 1 17–18)

It views the whole of creation as a sacred text in which wisdom is to be found. It studies the elements of earth, air, fire and water to discover hidden truths. As the Soothsayer in *Antony and Cleopatra* says, 'Nature's infinite book of secrecy' is to be read (*Antony* I 2 10). It is to be pored over like a holy book that will open its treasures to the enquiring spirit.

Lord Cerimon in *Pericles* is such a student of nature. He has studied what he calls 'the blest infusions that dwell in vegetives, in metals, stones'. He knows 'the disturbances that nature works, and of her cures' (*Pericles* III 2 34–7), and as a mage he uses this wisdom to heal, to bring back to life and restore. The healing graces of the mage are not opposed to nature. They are not supernatural or other than natural. Rather, they cooperate with nature. They reawaken us to the energies and relationships that are deepest and most natural.

When Lord Cerimon revives the body of Pericles' queen, whom it was thought had died at sea, he says, 'Nature awakes' (*Pericles* III 2 92). He has used his grace of wisdom not to dominate nature or to dictate to it but to liberate it, to set it free. The work of the mage in us is to restore what is natural. It is to heal the true nature of our lives, not to make us something other than ourselves. For Lord Cerimon this work of healing is of greater delight:

> Than to be thirsty after tottering honour,
> Or tie my pleasure up in silken bags,
> To please the fool and death.
>
> (*Pericles* III 2 39–41)

It is that part of us that longs more for well-being than wealth. It is that dimension of our soul that sees the value of wholeness over honours.

Pericles himself is restored to health, although it is not a simple return to what he was before but a transformation that incorporates the struggles and the suffering of his experiences. Healing comes to him in part through his dream life and through an attentiveness to 'the music of the spheres' (*Pericles* V 1 229). Listening at levels deeper than consciousness to the harmony of the stars in motion opens him further to the mystery of life. It awakens him to an awareness of the hidden relationship between all things. 'Such harmony is in immortal souls', as Lorenzo says in *The Merchant of Venice*, though 'we cannot hear it' (*Merchant* V 1 63–5). It is the harmony that we need to live in relation to. It cannot be sensed with our outward faculty of hearing but it is the score that underlies the whole of life. The mage in us is attentive to this harmony.

The Denial of Spirit

Unlike the seer and the mage there are those who are closed to the unseen. They take no notice of the interminglings of heaven and earth. They are as inattentive to the messages that come to us in our dreams as they are to the healing properties that lie hidden within plants, and just as the influence of the stars is ridiculed by them so is the inner realm of the unconscious. For them matter is not interwoven with spirit. The visible world is not threaded through with strands of the unseen. In *Romeo and Juliet* when the young Montague has a foreboding dream and a premonition of what he calls 'some consequence yet hanging in the stars' (*Romeo* I 4 107), his friend Mercutio responds cynically. Dreams, he says, 'are the children of an idle brain, begot of nothing but vain fantasy' (*Romeo* I 4 97–8).

Much more sinister in his ridiculing of the unknown is Edmund, the bastard son of Gloucester in *King Lear*, who is dismissive of unseen influences on our lives. Self-determination and the power of the will, he contends, is all that matters:

> This is the excellent foppery of the world, that when
> we are sick in fortune – often the surfeits of our own
> behaviour – we make guilty of our disasters the sun,
> the moon, and stars, as if we were villains on necessity,
> fools by heavenly compulsion, knaves, thieves, and
> treachers by spherical predominance, drunkards, liars,
> and adulterers by an enforced obedience of planetary
> influence; and all that we are evil in by a divine thrusting-
> on. An admirable evasion of whoremaster man, to lay
> his goatish disposition to the charge of a star. My father
> compounded with my mother under the Dragon's tail,
> and my nativity was under Ursa Major, so that it follows
> I am rough and lecherous. Fut! I should have been that
> I am had the maidenliest star in the firmament twinkled
> at my bastardizing.
>
> (*Lear* I 2 118–32)

Part of what Edmund is saying is true. We cannot deny responsibility for what we do. It is false, however, to pretend that there are not also countless unseen influences at work within us and around us in our lives, and that we are part of the interdependent web of the universe in both its seen and unseen strands.

What is it in us that closes down to the unknown? Is it simply that we are wary of the tendency to misread the unconscious or that we fear the strangeness of what cannot outwardly be handled? Certainly this is part of our hesitation, although the unseen will not become less strange to us if we deny our inner faculties of perception. In fact the opposite will be the case. The less we access the archetypal depths of the seer and mage in our souls the more frightening the realm of the unknown will become. Is the problem not that we tend to give our conscious side a monopoly of power, but that our ego finds it difficult to be guided by the unconscious in shaping our lives and relationships? We think it more straightforward to keep everything at the rational level. Our lives may thus be more straightforward but they also will be less integrated and at times less safe.

In *King Richard III* we find Hastings ridiculing Lord Stanley for being attentive to his dreams of the night. 'I wonder he's so simple', says Hastings, 'to trust the mockery of unquiet slumbers' (*Richard III* III 2 26–7). In the end, however, if Hastings had heeded the 'unquiet' of Stanley's dreams, he would have avoided the murderous plans of the king against him. Our conscious side alone is limited in its ability to know what threatens or feeds our well-being. There are times when it is only our inner faculty of knowing that will be able to perceive what is right or what is harmful in our lives.

In *Troilus and Cressida* the prophetess Cassandra is scorned for her 'brain-sick raptures', as Troilus calls them (*Troilus* II 2 123). Within herself she sees Troy's destruction, but the city and her family do not want to hear her prophetic words calling either for change or defeat. The play focuses on the personal tragedy of her brother Troilus and his rejection in love. He is absorbed by his relationship with Cressida and then by his loss of love when she betrays him. Engulfed in his own pain he is only half alive to what is happening to his besieged city. Increasingly he becomes enclosed in a private world of hurt and resentment. Cassandra sees more suffering coming, on a collective as well as a personal level. Troilus dismisses her as a 'foolish, dreaming, superstitious girl' (*Troilus* V 3 78). It is a picture of how woundedness in our lives, instead of cutting us further open to truth, sometimes can seal us off from truth. Our inner senses become overlaid, especially in relation to what we fear. The seer in our depths becomes blinkered.

Perhaps it is in Julius Caesar that we find the most tragic consequences of closing down to the unseen. As the conspiracy against him grows in the hearts of his assassins, a soothsayer in the capital senses danger and warns him, 'Beware the ides of March.' Caesar ignores the seer's warning. 'He is a dreamer. Let us leave him,' he says (*Julius* I 1 24). Caesar represents that side of us that is quick to deny the unknown, particularly when its warnings are unsettling. The signs, however, continue to break into his consciousness. During the night the elements are disturbed and, as he recounts, his wife has foreboding dreams,

> Nor heaven nor earth have been at peace tonight;
> Thrice hath Calpurnia in her sleep cried out,
> 'Help, ho! they murder Caesar!'

'The noise of battle hurtled in the air,' he says, 'horses did neigh' and 'ghosts did shriek'. Nevertheless Caesar chooses to ignore the signs and to attend the senate as usual the next day. 'Caesar shall go forth,' he asserts, 'for these predictions are to the world in general as to Caesar' (*Julius* II 2 1–29).

When his wife tells him further of her dream, that she has seen him as a statue 'which, like a fountain with an hundred spouts, did run pure blood' (*Julius* II 2 77–8), he momentarily relents. So ready is he to deny what is disturbing, however, that a reinterpretation of the dream easily comforts him. It is in fact one of the conspirators who assures him by saying,

> It was a vision fair and fortunate:
> Your statue spouting blood in many pipes . . .
> Signifies that from you great Rome shall suck
> Reviving blood.

> (*Julius* II 2 85–8)

Relieved that the dream has been flatteringly interpreted, Caesar concludes, 'this way have you well expounded it' (*Julius* II 2 91). He goes forth to the senate and dies at the hands of the assassins.

Haunted by the Unknown

Whereas Julius Caesar closes himself to the unseen, Prince Hamlet opens himself, but it is his grieving and bitter side that he opens. He becomes haunted and distressed by his exposure to the unknown. Even before he has seen the ghost of his murdered father, Hamlet is depressed. He wishes that 'the Everlasting' were not opposed to 'self-slaughter':

> . . . O God, God,
> How weary, stale, flat and unprofitable
> Seem to me all the uses of this world!
> Fie on't, ah, fie, 'tis an unweeded garden
> That grows to seed. Things rank and gross in nature
> Possess it merely.
>
> (*Hamlet* I 2 131–7)

And after he has seen the apparition of his murdered father, although he can still name the wonder of creation and the mystery of humanity, he says to Rosencrantz and Guildenstern,

> . . . This most excellent canopy, the air, look you, this
> brave o'erhanging firmament, this majestical roof fretted
> with golden fire – why, it appears nothing to me but a foul
> pestilent congregation of vapours. What a piece of work
> is man, how noble in reason, how infinite in faculties, in
> form and moving how express and admirable, in action
> how like an angel, in apprehension how like a god: the
> beauty of the world, the paragon of animals! And yet to
> me what is this quintessence of dust? Man delights not
> me – nor woman neither, though by your smiling you
> seem to say so.
>
> (*Hamlet* II 2 299–310)

So obsessed is he by what has gone wrong that he loses faith in the sacred act of procreation. Absorbed by his own failures and by the knowledge of what the hidden world has shown him, he says to his love Ophelia,

> Get thee to a nunnery. Why wouldst thou be a breeder
> of sinners? I am myself indifferent honest; but yet I could
> accuse me of such things that it were better my mother
> had not borne me. I am very proud, revengeful, ambitious,
> with more offences at my beck than I have thoughts to
> put them in, imagination to give them shape, or time to
> act them in. What should such fellows as I do crawling
> between earth and heaven? We are arrant knaves all.
> Believe none of us. Go thy ways to a nunnery.
>
> (*Hamlet* III 1 121-30)

The realm of the unseen has occupied his mind. The unconscious now dominates. He has been shaken by his father's death, and in his weakened state lacks the strength to integrate the known and the unknown. Instead of simply accessing the seer within himself, he allows it to take over.

All along, however, Hamlet knows that in the unseen there are both forces of light and powers of darkness, influences for good and principalities of destruction. When he sees the ghost he tries to discern its energies,

> Angels and ministers defend us!
> Be thou a spirit of health or goblin damned,
> Bring with thee airs from heaven or blasts from hell,
> Be thy intents wicked or charitable.
>
> (*Hamlet* I 4 39–42)

To say that within us there are archetypal depths of the seer is not to say that everything we see with the inner eye is from 'heaven'. We also can be exposed to 'blasts from hell', as Hamlet says. We can tune in to hidden life-giving streams in our souls. We can also hear horrifying and destructive impulses to wrong.

When the ghost confirms for Hamlet what already he has sensed within himself about his uncle's role in the death of his father, Hamlet says, 'O my prophetic soul!' (*Hamlet* I 5 40). Inwardly he has known all along what outwardly has not yet been proved. It is the capacity in us to intuit at levels deeper than external knowledge, to see within before we know without. Yet still Hamlet continues to test what the ghost and his 'prophetic soul' have communicated. He decides to use the court's visiting players to enact before his uncle a scene that will depict the ghost's version of his father's murder, for as Hamlet says,

> ... The spirit that I have seen
> May be a devil, and the devil hath power
> T'assume a pleasing shape, yea, and perhaps
> Out of my weakness and my melancholy,
> As he is very potent with such spirits,
> Abuses me to damn me: I'll have grounds
> More relative than this. The play's the thing
> Wherein I'll catch the conscience of the King.
>
> (*Hamlet* II 2 596–603)

Although Hamlet tests the unseen, and finds to his own satisfaction that his uncle is guilty, his experience of the unknown drives him into an obsession with the bitterness that already was in him, and eventually into a type of madness. Hamlet, of course, denies that he is mad. 'I am but mad north-north-west', he says. 'When the wind is southerly, I know a hawk from a handsaw' (*Hamlet* II 2 377–8). But that is a characteristic of most madness. Most people suffering from forms of insanity will believe at certain points that they are more sane than the rest of the world. To his mother he says, 'I essentially am not in madness, but mad in craft' (*Hamlet* III 4 188–9). It is those who are closest to him, however, his mother and Ophelia, who see the extent of the obsession that has gripped him. The Queen perceives he is 'mad as the sea and wind when both contend which is the mightier' (*Hamlet* IV 1 7–8). The struggle within him is between the unconscious and the conscious, between a sea of anger swelling from unknown depths and an uncertainty of mind as to what he should do. Ophelia believes that his reason has been 'o'erthrown' (*Hamlet* III 1 151). It is being dictated to by the obsessive rage in his soul. His mind, she says, is 'like sweet bells jangled, out of tune and harsh' (*Hamlet* III 1 158–62).

Yet there is a seeing in his madness or what Lord Polonius calls a 'method' in his madness. He hits on perceptions that 'reason and sanity' might miss (*Hamlet* II 2 205–11). The powerful surges of the unconscious in him produce sharp insights in the midst of his mental storm. He distinguishes, for instance, between his true self and his false self. He sees his destructive behaviour as issuing up from a haunted place within himself. Offering an apology to Laertes for insulting and wronging him at Ophelia's graveside, Hamlet says,

> Give me your pardon, sir. I have done you wrong.
> ... What I have done
> ... I here proclaim was madness.
> Was't Hamlet wronged Laertes? Never Hamlet.
> If Hamlet from himself be ta'en away,
> And when he's not himself does wrong Laertes,
> Then Hamlet does it not. Hamlet denies it.
> Who does it then? His madness. If't be so,
> Hamlet is of the faction that is wronged.
> His madness is poor Hamlet's enemy.
>
> (*Hamlet* V 2 220–33)

When we are not truly ourselves, or when we act in ways that are distant from our true depths, the wrongs we commit are an affront to those we violate. They are also an offence to our own souls. In the midst of his struggle with madness, Hamlet sees this.

The Shadow of the Unseen

Always in Hamlet there is a tension between love and hate, between goodness and wrongdoing, and even his bitterness is conceived out of a natural passion. It is the anger that a son naturally experiences when terrible wrong is done to his father. But there are characters who entirely give themselves over to the destructive powers of the unseen. Unlike the mage, whose intention is to restore and heal, the sorcerer on the other hand seeks to manipulate and to distort. Antipholus of Syracuse refers to them as 'dark-working sorcerers that change the mind' (*Comedy* I 2 99). It is that part of us that can engage with the unseen in order to oppose what is natural or to exert control over others and to misdirect them.

One such character is Joan of Arc or Joan La Pucelle as Shakespeare entitles her in *1 King Henry VI*. She counterfeits under the guise of having a 'spirit of deep prophecy' (*1 Henry VI* I 2 55). The reality is that she has given herself over to energies of the unseen for the sake of power. Speaking to the forces of darkness amidst a storm of thunder, she says, 'take my soul – my body, soul and all' (*1 Henry VI* V 3 22). Everything that is within her she offers up for the sake of political and military success. She represents the shadow side of the mage, the use of hidden knowledge for her own gain and her own glory.

One of the marks of this type of falseness is the compulsive desire to be more than 'common'. In the case of Joan La Pucelle it takes the form of denying her humble origins and claiming to be above natural appetites. Outwardly she professes to be a virgin, disdaining sexual relationship. In reality there are few French lords with whom she has not slept. She lies about her descent, professing to be of 'noble birth' (*1 Henry VI* V 4 22). In fact she is the daughter of a shepherd. When he comes to her at the time of her execution to offer a father's blessing, she rejects him calling him a 'base ignoble wretch' (*1 Henry VI* V 4 8). Her relationship with the unseen is driven by the desire to be other than herself. She represents the way in which self-shame leads us, whether consciously or unconsciously, to a denial of our deepest identity. It seizes the shadow form of any of the archetypes to cover the nakedness of our origins.

Perhaps the most distorted example of sorcery, with its manipulation of the unseen, occurs in *Macbeth*. As the three witches intone at the beginning of the play, 'Fair is foul, and foul is fair' (*Macbeth* I 1 9). It is the perverted exchange of goodness for evil, and truth for falsehood. Even the appearance of the witches speaks of the distortion of what is natural. As Macbeth's companion Banquo says to them,

> ... You should be women;
> And yet your beards forbid me to interpret
> That you are so.
>
> (*Macbeth* I 3 44–6)

And just as their appearance is unnatural, so is their prophetic greeting. It is the speaking of half-truths designed to mislead Macbeth onto a path that will take him further and further from his true self.

When it appears that their auguries, including the prophetic announcement that Macbeth is Thane of Cawdor, have a degree of truth about them, Banquo asks, 'Can the devil speak true?' (*Macbeth* I 3 107). He suspects, however, that there is more falseness in the witches than truth, and he warns Macbeth,

> ... oftentimes, to win us to our harm,
> The instruments of darkness tell us truths;
> Win us with honest trifles, to betray's
> In deepest consequence.
>
> (*Macbeth* I 3 122–5)

Our capacity to see at levels deeper than outward sight is great. We also are capable of great delusion, and the latter often happens because of the particles of light that we glimpse amidst what is largely shadow.

Lady Macbeth is immediately vulnerable to the temptation of the prophecy. If Macbeth will be king, she will be queen. But the lie of the tragedy is not slow to emerge when she says to Macbeth,

> ... to be more than what you were, you would
> Be so much more the man.
>
> (*Macbeth* I 7 50–1)

It is the lie of our lives when we desire to become something 'more' than ourselves. It is the tragedy of our cultures and religious traditions when we begin to believe that happiness will be attained by becoming something other than ourselves, striving to conform to an image that is not our true self.

The whole direction of the tragedy now is the movement of

Macbeth and Lady Macbeth away from what is most original in themselves. They are consumed by fighting their own nature, and by denying the most natural features of human relationship. Lady Macbeth is impatient at the goodness that persists in showing itself in Macbeth's character. His nature 'is too full o' the milk of human-kindness', she says (*Macbeth* I 5 15). He needs to be more ambitious for the crown. She on the other hand is consumed by ambition. In contemplating the murder of King Duncan, Lady Macbeth allows herself to be taken over by the destructive energies of the unseen,

> . . . Come, you spirits
> That tend on mortal thoughts, unsex me here
> And fill me from the crown to the toe top-full
> Of direst cruelty. Make thick my blood;
> Stop up the access and passage to remorse,
> That no compunctious visitings of nature
> Shake my fell purpose, nor keep peace between
> The effect and it. Come to my woman's breasts
> And take my milk for gall, you murdering ministers,
> Wherever, in your sightless substances
> You wait on nature's mischief. Come, thick night,
> And pall me in the dunnest smoke of hell,
> That my keen knife see not the wound it makes,
> Nor heaven peep through the blanket of the dark,
> To cry 'Hold, hold!'
>
> (*Macbeth* I 5 38–52)

She becomes more and more unnatural and counsels her husband to do the same. 'Look like the innocent flower,' she says, 'but be the serpent under't' (*Macbeth* I 5 63–4) for 'false face must hide what the false heart doth know' (*Macbeth* I 7 82). She represents the denial of natural simplicity, yet the truly natural keeps trying to assert itself in her. She in fact finds it impossible to stab the sleeping King Duncan because he reminds her of her own father,

> . . . Had he not resembled
> My father as he slept, I had done't.
>
> (*Macbeth* II 2 11–12)

Nature provides us with a sense of relationship. Unnatural desire tears it apart, but even as it is torn apart our most natural instincts for relationship call out to be heard.

Macbeth murders the king in the night. It is the turning point of his descent into self-destruction. In the bedchamber of the murdered king he hears someone calling out in their sleep, 'God bless us'. He finds, however, that he cannot say 'Amen'. 'I had most need of blessing,' he says, 'and "Amen" stuck in my throat' (*Macbeth* II 2 32–3). His falseness separates him from benediction. The obstacle is the unnaturalness of his deed. He begins to experience the correlation between unnaturalness and lack of blessing. It is the relationship that now haunts his life.

Macbeth also thinks he hears a voice crying,

> . . . 'Sleep no more!
> Macbeth does murder sleep' – the innocent sleep,
> Sleep that knits up the ravelled sleave of care,
> The death of each day's life, sore labour's bath,
> Balm of hurt minds, great nature's second course,
>
> (*Macbeth* II 2 36–41)

He 'hath murdered sleep', continues the voice, and 'shall sleep no more, Macbeth shall sleep no more' (*Macbeth* II 2 43–4). Part of the curse of unnaturalness is that it separates us from the rhythms of rest and renewal. Deep in the created order are patterns of stillness and sleep. They are woven into creation in relation to activity and wakefulness. Without nature's gift of rest at night we are only half alive to the delights and demands of the day. Macbeth has murdered the source of his own renewal. He will no longer experience stillness in his soul. As one of the Scottish lords says of the false king later in the play, 'all that is within him does condemn itself for being there' (*Macbeth* V 2 24–5). Macbeth's inner being now is perpetually in turmoil. In his wickedness there is no rest for him.

Lady Macbeth also experiences a condemnation in her soul of what she has done and become. She is haunted by her inhumanity. To begin with, as they washed the murdered king's blood from their hands, she had said,

> A little water clears us of this deed;
> How easy is it then!
>
> (*Macbeth* II 2 67–8)

By the end, however, she is compulsively rubbing her hands as if trying to rid them of the blood. 'Out, damned spot! Out, I say!'

(*Macbeth* V 1 34) but to no avail. 'Here's the smell of the blood still', she says. 'All the perfumes of Arabia will not sweeten this little hand' (*Macbeth* V 1 48–9). Nothing releases her from the memory of the falseness. She lives in a terrified inner imprisonment. Frightened of the dark she insists always on a candle by her side. Her soul is no longer a sanctuary. It is a chamber of fear and condemnation.

To follow hidden destructive energies within ourselves, and thus to become distant from the true centre of our souls, is also to be displaced from the inner foundations of our security. No sooner has Macbeth achieved kingship than he begins to fear that it will be taken from him. Even his closest friend becomes a focus of his crippling anxiety,

> To be thus is nothing;
> But to be safely thus! – Our fears in Banquo
> Stick deep; and in his royalty of nature
> Reigns that which would be feared.
>
> (*Macbeth* III 1 47–50)

Macbeth sees Banquo's 'royalty of nature' but knows nothing of it in himself. He now arranges the murder of his friend and plants spies in the household of every Scottish thane.

As Hecat, the queen of darkness, says to the three witches in appearing to them from the realm of the unknown,

> ...you all know security
> Is mortals' chiefest enemy.
>
> (*Macbeth* III 5 32–3)

Macbeth has lost his inner security because he has abandoned his true self. He lacks confidence because he has deserted the stronghold of his own being. His 'chiefest enemy' now is his uncertainty of where safety is to be found. In a desperate search for assurance he returns to the witches, the original source of his confusions. Again they offer him falseness clothed in a perversion of truth,

> Be bloody, bold, and resolute; laugh to scorn
> The power of man; for none of woman born
> Shall harm Macbeth. ...
> Be lion-mettled, proud; and take no care
> Who chafes, who frets, or where conspirers are;

> Macbeth shall never vanquished be until
> Great Birnam Wood to high Dunsinane Hill
> Shall come against him.
>
> (*Macbeth* IV 1 78–93)

The full truth, of course, which Macbeth does not perceive until the end, is that 'Great Birnam Wood' does travel to Dunsinane because its trees are cut down to be carried as camouflage by Scotland's liberating army. And Macduff, who eventually slays Macbeth, is not 'of woman born' because at his birth he had been delivered by caesarean section, torn prematurely from his mother's womb. Macbeth's encounters with the unknown have misled him with half-truths.

Throughout his descent into self-destruction the torment of Macbeth's inner world is reflected in an outward chaos in the world of his relationships and nation. As early as the night of King Duncan's murder there is a prophetic correspondence between the elements of creation in a wildness of storm and Macbeth's forsaking of truth in his soul. As one of the Scottish lords recounts,

> ... Where we lay,
> Our chimneys were blown down, and ...
> Lamentings heard i'the air, strange screams of death,
> And prophesying, with accents terrible,
> Of dire combustion and confused events
> New-hatched to the woeful time. The obscure bird
> Clamoured the live-long night. Some say the earth
> Was feverous and did shake.
>
> (*Macbeth* II 3 51–8)

Macbeth's inner abandonment of true human nature is mirrored by a disturbance in the natural world. There is a correlation between what happens in our souls and the well-being of creation and human relationship.

As the doctor caring for Lady Macbeth says, 'unnatural deeds do breed unnatural troubles' (*Macbeth* V 1 67–8). Falseness perverts the natural order of relationship. Macbeth, formerly the friend of Scotland, becomes instead the 'fiend of Scotland' (*Macbeth* IV 3 232), tearing apart the life of the nation that before he had served. Macduff in exile says,

> ... Each new morn
> New widows howl, new orphans cry, new sorrows
> Strike heaven on the face.
>
> (*Macbeth* IV 3 4–6)

The country 'weeps, it bleeds; and each new day a gash is added to her wounds' (*Macbeth* IV 3 40-1). The neglect and manipulation of truth in the realm of the unknown wreaks havoc in the life of the nation.

Always there is the inexplicable 'why?' in relation to acts of such inhumanity and unnatural cruelty. What is it that compels the shadow of the seer and mage in the human spirit to so distort and manipulate truth? Macbeth, in his very first encounter with the witches, asks them,

> . . . Say from whence
> You owe this strange intelligence; or why
> Upon this blasted heath you stop our way
> With such prophetic greetings? Speak, I charge you!
> (*Macbeth* I 3 74-7)

But Macbeth never is told, nor does he receive a clear response to a similar question during his final encounter with the witches. He asks them what they are doing. 'A deed without a name', they reply (*Macbeth* IV 1 48). The dark wrongs that we are part of in our lives, or that we witness in our world, are beyond neat explanation. Their source is never made plain. We can know within ourselves when we are in the presence of such wrong, or when we have given way to unnatural energy in our lives and relationships, but we cannot reduce this awareness to the boundaries of comprehension. It is 'without a name'.

Having given himself over to the namelessness of evil, Macbeth enters a final meaninglessness. On hearing of Lady Macbeth's death, he says,

> . . . Out, out, brief candle!
> Life's but a walking shadow, a poor player
> That struts and frets his hour upon the stage
> And then is heard no more. It is a tale
> Told by an idiot, full of sound and fury,
> Signifying nothing.
> (*Macbeth* V 5 23-8)

Having deserted his true self in order to become someone other than himself, Macbeth is consumed by life's shadow. In the end he believes in nothing.

The Salvific Mage

Whereas Macbeth represents a loss of order and a loss of meaning, Prospero on the other hand, the great mage of *The Tempest*, represents a restoring of order and a recovery of meaning. Even before being wrongfully ousted from his Dukedom of Milan, Prospero had been 'rapt in secret studies' (*Tempest* I 2 76), searching for truths hidden from outward sight. It is not, however, until the personal sufferings of his exile that he begins to harness his knowledge for the work of liberation and healing, which is the essential vocation of the mage. *The Tempest* is about the reawakening of true human nature.

Prospero as mage cooperates with the unseen energies of earth, air and sea in his magical work of transformation. Ariel, a spirit of the air, whom Prospero had set free from imprisonment in a pine tree, is his principal workmate. Together they achieve the major events of the play which are a restoration of Prospero to the Dukedom of Milan and a redemption of those who have wronged him. Like the magi in the Christmas story who are attentive to a guiding star, Prospero discerns 'a most auspicious star' (*Tempest* I 2 183) under which the events of this salvific drama unfold.

Antonio, the usurping Duke of Milan, and those who have aided him in his falseness, are driven by storm to the coastline of Prospero's island of exile and are shipwrecked. In the air above them Ariel says,

> . . . you three
> From Milan did supplant good Prospero;
> Exposed unto the sea, which hath requit it,
> Him and his innocent child; for which foul deed
> The powers, delaying, not forgetting, have
> Incensed the seas and shores, yea, all the creatures,
> Against your peace.

> (*Tempest* III 3 69–75)

The picture is of the powers of creation, both seen and unseen, having a type of memory of the wrongs that were done years before. Their judgement has been delayed but not forgotten. The mage's role is to help awaken that memory and to focus its energies of retribution. The judgement, however, is not for the punishing of those who have done wrong. Rather it is for their repentance and transformation. No one is harmed in the shipwreck. Even their garments remain unstained, and as one of the company says,

> ...there is in this business more than nature
> Was ever conduct of.
>
> (*Tempest* V 1 245–6)

The collaboration between creation and the mage is that of nature and grace working in cooperation. This is a major feature of the archetype of the mage. The mage stands not over and against nature, manipulating it and dictating, but alongside nature, knowing its secrets and releasing its powerful forces for good.

The shipwrecked party begin to hear echoed in the elements the wrongs they have done to Prospero and his daughter Miranda. The King of Naples says,

> Methought the billows spoke and told me of it;
> The winds did sing it to me, and the thunder,
> That deep and dreadful organ pipe, pronounced
> The name of Prosper.
>
> (*Tempest* III 3 96–9)

With the power of the storm speaking against them, they begin to repent. Prospero immediately calls off the tempest. It has done its work,

> ...The rarer action is
> In virtue than in vengeance. They being penitent
> The sole drift of my purpose doth extend
> Not a frown further. Go release them, Ariel.
> My charms I'll break, their senses I'll restore,
> And they shall be themselves.
>
> (*Tempest* V 1 27–32)

'And they shall be themselves.' This is the vision of the mage, that we shall be ourselves. This is the hope of the archetypal energies of the mage in us, that creation shall be restored to itself, that we and all things will be released from the falseness of what we have become. Even Caliban the savage, who represents the human capacity to become little more than a beast, moves in the end towards a type of repentance. 'I'll be wise hereafter and seek for grace', he says (*Tempest* V 1 298–9).

In the final words of the epilogue Prospero says that it is forgiveness that has the power to set us free,

> ...my ending is despair
> Unless I be relieved by prayer,
> Which pierces so that it assaults
> Mercy itself, and frees all faults.
> As you from crimes would pardoned be,
> Let your indulgence set me free.
>
> (*Tempest* Epilogue 15–20)

But the setting free of others is not something that the mage does without also awakening in them an awareness of the wrongs they have done. Throughout the play there is a recurring theme of awareness. As Ariel sings to the shipwrecked party,

> If of life you keep a care,
> Shake off slumber, and beware.
> Awake, awake!
>
> (*Tempest* II 1 305–7)

The work of the mage is to wake us to the truth of what is within us and around us. It is a waking also to the falseness of what is within our lives and to our complicity in wrong. At one point the mage of *The Tempest* orchestrates a great pinching of the offenders as they stand in a charmed circle into which he has drawn them. These are 'inward pinches', he says (*Tempest* V 1 76). It is a nipping of their inner awareness, to waken them to themselves.

The Tempest is a play about restoration. Part of the redemption is a restoring of Prospero's dukedom. He recognizes, however, that it, like all things, is passing. Nothing that we outwardly know is to be clutched after and tightly held, for all of these things are temporary. There will be a time when they are no more. They are expressions of what we cannot see, echoes of what cannot yet be heard. This includes even the knowledge and the practice of the mage's art. This too is passing, and so when Prospero completes his task he says,

> ...this rough magic
> I here abjure...
> ...I'll break my staff,
> Bury it certain fathoms in the earth,

And deeper than did ever plummet sound
I'll drown my book.

(Tempest V 1 50–7)

His book of wisdom he casts into the sea. It is like the sea of the unconscious. Its treasure will be found again by others. Its contents will wash up here and there onto the shores of consciousness but now in his own life he will let go of it. And in his return as an old man to the Dukedom of Milan he will prepare for his own passing. 'Every third thought', he says, 'shall be my grave' (*Tempest* V 1 315).

This is not a morbidness in the mage. Rather it is a clarity of vision. The mage knows the impermanence of all that can be seen. He is aware even that all our knowledge will pass. As Prospero stands with his prospective son-in-law, when together they have witnessed the dance of the spirits and their sudden vanishing from outward sight, he says,

> . . . These our actors
> . . . were all spirits and
> Are melted into air, into thin air;
> And, like the baseless fabric of this vision,
> The cloud-capped towers, the gorgeous palaces,
> The solemn temples, the great globe itself,
> Yea, all which it inherit, shall dissolve,
> And, like this unsubstantial pageant faded,
> Leave not a rack behind. We are such stuff
> As dreams are made on, and our little life
> Is rounded with a sleep.

(Tempest IV 1 148–58)

The mage in us knows that just as what is seen comes forth from what is unseen, so in the end all that is visible will return to what is invisible. The healing of our lives is given not that we may avoid this passing. Rather it is given to prepare us for our return into the unknown.

V

The Fool and the Contemplative

*'All that lives must die, passing through nature
to eternity.'*
(*Hamlet* I 2 72–3)

All Things Passing

Every age has had its equivalent of the fool, whether that be the jester, the clown or the comedian. They are the ones who get us laughing at ourselves. They break through the veneers of self-importance and pretension. Their presence usually causes discomfort as well as laughter, for they tend to say the unsayable and to expose our insecurities. They ridicule the powerful, even though often it is the latter who employ them. They get away with a lot, for there is something in the human mystery that knows its need of the fool.

Similarly every culture has had its version of the contemplative – the hermit, the friar, the solitary – although certain cultures have been less tolerant than others of the contemplative's commitment to silence and detachment. Disciplines of disengagement allow for a perspective that cannot be obtained in the midst of life's busyness. It is a way of seeing that challenges the norms of family life and society, as well as consoling those who have been scarred by relationship and by life's demands. Those of us who have chosen not to follow the traditional path of solitude can at the same time know that our perspective on life is limited when we view things only from the place of busy engagement. And so again and again the insights of the contemplative have been sought.

The Russian tradition of the holy fool combines the archetypes of the fool and the contemplative. Even when they are not combined, however, we can detect a commonality between the two. Their shared starting point is that all things are passing. The fool knows and names that we are going to die. Everything is transitory, including the dignities and distinctions of life. This gives the fool a detachment of spirit, which is part of his gift of humour. What is your name, asks the judge of the fool in *Measure for Measure*. 'Bum', says the fool (*Measure* II 1 206). One name is as good as another, for all titles are passing.

In *As You Like It* when the fool Touchstone observes that it is ten o'clock in the morning, he says,

> Thus we may see . . . how the world wags:
> 'Tis but an hour ago since it was nine,
> And after one hour more 'twill be eleven;

And so from hour to hour we ripe, and ripe,
And then from hour to hour we rot, and rot;
And thereby hangs a tale.

(*As You* II 7 23–8)

The fool is a touchstone, a marker for the journey. His tale to everyone, whether king or cobbler, duchess or shepherd, is the same. Life
as we know it is impermanent. Everything outwardly that we try to
hold on to will disintegrate. We forget the fool's message even though
it is such an obvious perception. We try to deny the fool's wisdom
even though it is part of our own archetypal depths. Why?

In one sense the message of the fool is incontrovertible. We all
know that we are going to die. We know that one day everything
we see will be no more. Even the queen in *Hamlet*, who is so
attached to the outward trappings of royalty, knows it. 'All that
lives must die,' she says, 'passing through nature to eternity'
(*Hamlet* I 2 72–3). Like the queen, however, although we may
know it, it is more difficult to live it. We may be aware that all
things are passing but we end up clutching them to ourselves as
if they were forever. We know that our properties and possessions, like our titles and ranks, are impermanent but we wrap
our identities in them as if there were nothing else. We deceive
ourselves like the drunken Sir Toby Belch in *Twelfth Night* who
sings in one of his revels, 'I will never die'. In response the fool
sings, 'Sir Toby, there you lie' (*Twelfth* II 3 103–4).

The fool in us perceives self-deception and attempts to draw it
to our attention. Our conscious side, however, does not always find
this easy, for part of the fool's tale is that consciousness itself is
passing. The ego is being told that one day it will be no more, a
truth that is difficult to face. And so the fool sidesteps
confrontation by using wit and humour to make the point. This is
not to say that the ego will always accept being humoured.
Sometimes our conscious side simply bans the fool so as not to
have to hear uncomfortable truths.

Jaques in *As You Like It* says that the fool has 'strange places
crammed with observation' (*As You* II 7 40–1). His observations
on life are with a lightness of touch, but he sees from a rich depth
that can seem 'strange' or unfamiliar. The fool is 'deep-contem-
plative', says Jaques (*As You* II 7 31). His energies merge with
those of the contemplative, for part of knowing what is deep in life
is to know also what is not deep. Part of knowing where our true
security lies is to name where it does not lie. In that sense the fool
prepares the way for the contemplative. The perspective of the

fool can free us from imprisonments at the surface of life so that we can dive into its deeper currents.

The common starting point for the fool and the contemplative is the recognition that all things are passing. In *Twelfth Night* the friar measures time in terms of the distance between the present and the grave. This is not a gloomy melancholy in the friar. Rather it is an awareness, similar to what we have noted in the fool, of the transitoriness of life. The contemplative, however, is alert not simply to the transient nature of things. He is alive also to what is not passing. The contemplative looks to the mystery that is deeper than death, to the eternity out of which life comes forth. He notices the new beginnings that can emerge out of endings and the births that are born out of pain. In *The Comedy of Errors* the Abbess of Ephesus thinks she has lost her entire family. When she finds them again, she says, 'After so long grief, such nativity' (*Comedy* V 1 407). The contemplative knows 'grief' but believes in 'nativity'. It is that part of our soul that experiences pain in the loss of what is dear to us while at the same time trusting in what is not yet born.

We live much of the time in a denial of death's powers. We avert our gaze from the passing of life. In *2 King Henry VI* the Duchess of Gloucester, as she contemplates her imprisonment and encroaching demise, says that throughout her life she has feared the word death because of her longings for what she calls 'this world's eternity' (*2 Henry VI* II 4 90). She has tried to live as if this world, with its privileges and distinctions, were everlasting. Her contemplative side has been suppressed. In the midst of loss, however, it is born again from within her. She begins to see with a perspective that had been almost entirely dulled in her life.

Part of the denial of death is our fear of the unknown. This includes our dread of decomposing bodily. In *Measure for Measure* Claudio, facing a death sentence, says,

> Death is a fearful thing. . . .
> . . . to die, and go we know not where;
> To lie in cold obstruction and to rot;
> This sensible warm motion to become
> A kneaded clod; . . .
> The weariest and most loathed worldly life
> That age, ache, penury and imprisonment
> Can lay on nature is a paradise
> To what we fear of death.

> (*Measure* III 1 119–35)

The degree to which we neglect the contemplative within ourselves is the degree to which our fears fasten onto the physical side of death. In the absence of contemplation we notice only what is passing. We see the prospect of our body rotting but we miss the unseen root of our being.

When Sir John Falstaff is encouraged to start mending his life before his 'old body' gives out, he says, 'Peace, ... do not bid me remember mine end' (*2 Henry IV* II 4 229–30). If in our 'end' we see nothing other than the passing of our bodies, then the contemplative in us has been suppressed. Falstaff represents such a suppression. He has defined his life in terms of physical gratification. His death, therefore, can seem nothing more to him than the end. It is difficult for him to contemplate death as a return into the unseen if for him the unseen has not existed in his life.

When the contemplative dimension of our being has been neglected, not only is death an uncomfortable subject, so also is any reference to the unseen. When eventually Falstaff does come to his deathbed and is so close to the final moment that he calls out, 'God, God, God', his old friend Mistress Quickly of the Eastcheap Tavern later recounts,

> Now I, to comfort him, bid him 'a should not think
> of God – I hoped there was no need to trouble himself
> with any such thoughts yet.
>
> (*Henry V* II 3 18–21)

For the non-contemplative a recognition of the mystery of the unseen is denied almost at any cost, and certainly until the last possible moment. If awareness of the unseen has not been a feature of one's life, why bother with it while one is still breathing?

It is the same Mistress Quickly who in *The Merry Wives of Windsor* says of one of her fellow house-servants that although he is an honest fellow, 'his worst fault is that he is given to prayer. He is something peevish that way' (*Merry* I 4 12). Prayer, whether strident or quiet in its style, represents an awareness of the mystery. It is irksome to the person who would prefer not to be aware. The act of prayer presupposes that life is gift, that it has come forth from the invisible and will return to the invisible. It thus reminds us that as we were born so we will die.

The focus of the contemplative, however, is not just on the final moment. The focus is on dying in order to live. It is about how we let go of every moment and every day as much as how we let go of our final breath. It is about forgetting the past in order to remember the present, about letting go of cherished moments so that we can be open to this moment and to every moment that we are given. In *Measure for Measure* the Duke, disguised as a friar and commenting on the challenge of facing death, says, 'In this life lie hid more thousand deaths' (*Measure* III 1 39–40). Greater than the challenge of facing the final moment is how from day to day we let go of what is passing now. The archetype of the contemplative offers us a liberating strength. It is the strength to let go of what is known and secure in order to receive what is new and unknown. Both the contemplative and the fool point to a radical freedom.

Part of their freedom is the liberty to identify with whomever they wish, whether rich or poor, respected or condemned. The fool in *King Lear* says to Lear's old friend who has been locked up in the stocks for his loyalty to the king,

> That sir which serves and seeks for gain,
> And follows but for form,
> Will pack when it begins to rain,
> And leave thee in the storm;
> But I will tarry; the fool will stay,
> And let the wise man fly.

> (*Lear* II 4 74–9)

The fool has died to a dependence on outward respectability. He is free to identify with the accepted or the rejected. The wise man of the world, on the other hand, who builds his life on the foundations of external recognition finds himself trapped by its design, for a major part of its architecture is what is socially acceptable. He has sold his freedom. He has fallen out of touch with the fool in himself, which knows that the value of a person is based not on their outward markings but on the undefinable core of their being.

In *All's Well That Ends Well* the fool says, 'I am for the house with the narrow gate, which I take to be too little for pomp to enter' (*All's Well* IV 5 48–50). The way of the fool is a humble way. It calls for being close to the earth, for not being propped up by position and status. It is also a costly way for it does not heed the price. The fool weighs words and actions not by how easily they are uttered, nor by how readily they will be received, but by their truthfulness. Most people, says the fool, choose 'the flowery way that leads to the broad gate and the great fire' (*All's Well* IV 5 48–53). To ignore the way of the fool in our depths may seem the easy path. In the end, however, we are consumed by denial.

All of this is not to say that the fool goes out of his way to tread the hard path. He does not seek suffering. In fact he is keen to avoid it. In *Troilus and Cressida* when the fool Thersites flees from battle and is challenged to turn and fight by the bastard son of the king of Troy, he comically tries to find the common ground between himself and his pursuer. 'I am a bastard too', he says. 'I love bastards. I am ... in every thing illegitimate. One bear will not bite another, and wherefore should one bastard?' (*Troilus* V 7 16–19). The fool in us does not have a death instinct. It is that part of us that is prepared to choose 'the narrow gate' but not because of a longing for hardship. It is because of a preference for truth and for the inner freedom that accompanies truth.

Prince Hamlet in his madness shows some of the marks of the fool, although never with quite as light a touch. After the killing of Polonius, when Claudius asks him where Polonius is, Hamlet replies,

> At supper. ...
> Not where he eats, but where 'a is eaten. A certain
> convocation of politic worms are e'en at him. Your
> worm is your only emperor for diet. We fat all
> creatures else to fat us, and we fat ourselves for
> maggots. Your fat king and your lean beggar is but
> variable service – two dishes, but to one table. That's the end.
> (*Hamlet* IV 3 17–24)

It is the fool in us that knows we are all heading towards that 'supper'. Always in Hamlet, however, there is the shadow. He is making the fool's point, that all things are passing, but it is not with the detachment of the fool. Hamlet is driven and even possessed by his desire for revenge. Within himself he is not free.

Although there is always something of the shadow in Hamlet's foolishness, his contemplative side at times shines clearly. It is as if he is released momentarily from his consuming bitterness and in that moment is reacquainted with the contemplative in himself. 'There's a divinity that shapes our ends,' he says, 'rough-hew them how we will' (*Hamlet* V 2 10–11). He glimpses the larger picture. He sees the great current that carries us towards our end, noting also our tendency to resist the flow and our varied attempts at redirecting it. In pondering the possibility of his own death, he says,

> There is a special providence in the fall of a sparrow.
> If it be now, 'tis not to come. If it be not to come, it will
> be now. If it be not now, yet it will come. The readiness is all.
> (*Hamlet* V 2 214–16)

This is a major feature of the contemplative's message, as it is of the fool's. If death does not come now for us, it will come eventually. And so, as he says, 'the readiness is all'. It is the readiness to face one's final moment, but it is also the readiness in every moment to let go of what is passing in order to be alive to the new thing that is forever emerging within us and around us. This is the heart's desire of the fool and the contemplative. It is also the desire deep within the human soul for it is archetypal. It is part of our hope to be free.

The Freedom of the Fool

In *Twelfth Night* the fool says,

> ... He that is well hanged in this
> world needs fear no colours.

> (*Twelfth* I 5 4–5)

Those who have let go of their worries about outward status and possessions, or the men and women who have died to their anxieties about appearances and acceptance, are liberated in their own spirits. They need 'fear no colours', as the fool says. The flags of respectability, or the insignia of society's fashions, cannot intimidate them. External forces have lost their power.

Jaques in *As You Like It* aspires to be a fool. He likes the idea of freedom. 'I must have liberty', he says, 'as large a charter as the wind, to blow on whom I please; for so fools have' (*As You* II 7 47–9). But while he wants the freedom of a fool, his ego in fact is too dominating for him to let go to those depths within himself. And because he has not let go, his words are not liberating. They serve the speaker more than they serve the hearer. In his seven ages of man speech, Jaques cynically moves from the infant 'mewling and puking' through the different stages of life to the end which is 'mere oblivion', he says, 'sans teeth, sans eyes, sans taste, sans everything' (*As You* II 7 166–7). In the words of Jaques life is not simply passing, it is pathetic. His perspective grows not out of a freedom of spirit but out of a depressed spirit. When later in the play he is described as a 'melancholy fellow', Jaques responds, 'I am so: I do love it better than laughing' (*As You* IV 1 4). The shadow of the fool closes him down to life rather than opening him up. It leads him further away from others rather than drawing him closer.

The true fool may be driven away by those who want to banish truth but the nature of the fool is to choose to be among us, seeking our company and releasing our laughter. Despite the fun, however, the fool's message often is shoved aside. In *King Lear* the fool says, 'Truth's a dog must to kennel' (*Lear* I 4 110). We put truth in the doghouse when it becomes offensive. Lear's fool observes that a respectable lady can stand by the fireplace and make terrible smells, but if the dog does the same he is whipped and sent out to the shed. The fool has no power except truth. There is no outward security for the fool, other than whether or not people want his presence.

It is falseness that feels most threatened in the company of the fool. In *King Lear* one of the faithless daughters, Gonerill, is uneasy around her father's 'all-licensed fool', as she calls him (*Lear* I 4 196). She would prefer that he be censored. Truth is uncomfortable to her. Similarly the self-preoccupied Malvolio in *Twelfth Night* calls the fool 'a barren rascal' (*Twelfth* I 5 78). He would like a lid put on the fool. 'O, you are sick of self-love, Malvolio,' says the fool's patron, 'and taste with a distempered appetite. ... There is no slander in an allowed fool' (*Twelfth* I 5 85–9). When the fool within us speaks, it is not to misrepresent another. It is not to slander or insult. Rather it is to hold up the mirror and invite a true seeing.

While the fool sometimes is supported by kings and countesses, any patronage that comes must be without strings attached. There is to be no manipulating of the truth. In *Timon of Athens* the fool refuses a gift from the wealthy Timon because he sees the latter blinding himself to reality,

> No, I'll nothing. For if I should be bribed too,
> there would be none left to rail upon thee, and then
> thou wouldst sin the faster.

> (*Timon* I 2 243–5)

The fool attempts to hold up the truth to Timon, to warn him that he is being used for his wealth. Timon rejects the advice. He wants to believe that those who gather around him truly like him. As the fool observes, we are 'to counsel deaf, but not to flattery' (*Timon* I 2 253–4). We tend to struggle with the message of the fool when it challenges our ego. We avoid it both within ourselves and without.

Eventually Timon sees the truth, but not until his wealth is lost and his 'varnished friends' have deserted him. He flees from

Athens, embittered with humanity, to live with the beasts in the woods. He has swung from a naivety in human relationship to a hateful suspicion of everything human. His anger takes the form also of self-hatred. 'Thou hast cast away thyself', says the fool (*Timon* IV 3 221). In hating humanity he also is hating himself. In rejecting the whole of Athens he is recoiling from his own depths and from his own shadow. The fool criticizes him not because he is living with the beasts, for the beasts, as he says, are at least true to themselves. It is humanity that has the capacity to be false to itself. Timon has been part of that falseness but in experiencing it he projects his hatred entirely outwards. He chooses not to know himself.

The fool knows what is in the human heart and names it for us. In *Troilus and Cressida* when the fool is asked who he is, he says, 'Thy knower' (*Troilus* II 3 47). Like the purpose of the actor which Hamlet outlines to his visiting theatre company, it is 'to hold, as 'twere, the mirror up to nature' (*Hamlet* III 2 21–2). It is to reflect the truth and the falseness of the human spirit, to be an image of what is good in us and of what is distorted. The fool in our depths invites us to know ourselves.

In *As You Like It* Jaques says that the words of the fool are like a medicine to 'cleanse the foul body of th'infected world' (*As You* II 7 60). His words are spoken to all, whether high or low, whether friend or foe. They are designed to expose delusions and to pierce with truth. King Lear, after unwisely relinquishing power to his faithless daughters, is told that he has made his daughters his mothers. 'Thou gavest them the rod', says the fool, 'and puttest down thine own breeches' (*Lear* I 4 169–70). The commander of the Greek army is told that 'he has not so much brain as ear-wax' (*Troilus* V 1 49). The judge who asks the fool if prostitution is lawful is told, 'if the law would allow it' (*Measure* II 1 216). To the condemned prisoner, who is too drunk to wake up on his day of execution, the fool says, 'awake till you are executed, and sleep afterwards' (*Measure* IV 3 30–1). Concerning the person who is too full of his own opinion and likes to hear himself speak, the fool mimicks, 'I am Sir Oracle, and when I ope my lips, let no dog bark!' (*Merchant* I 1 93–4). And to the religious who are overly zealous about conversion, the fool says to the Jewess who has become a Christian, 'This making of Christians will raise the price of hogs' (*Merchant* III 5 22–3). Whatever we take too seriously, whether it is ourselves or our institutions or traditions, the fool ridicules.

Even the lowest in the social order does not escape the fool's

humour. In *As You Like It* Touchstone challenges the com-
placency even of a simple shepherd,

> Why, if thou never wast at court, thou never sawest
> good manners; if thou never sawest good manners,
> then thy manners must be wicked; and wickedness is
> sin, and sin is damnation. Thou art in a parlous state,
> shepherd.
>
> (*As You* III 2 38–42)

The shepherd lives in the idyllic Forest of Arden, well away from
the intrigue and corruption of the court, but his innocence and
naivety do not preclude him from the levelling wit of the fool. No
one is beyond poking fun at. No one should be left feeling too
secure outwardly.

One of the fool's universal themes is sex. It is an energy in every
human being and therefore a focus for the unsettling commentary
of the fool. Touchstone picks up on it in his conversation with the
shepherd. The latter may have a straightforward approach to the
breeding of creatures but likely it is based on received custom
rather than conscious reflection. The fool loves to provoke doubt in
relation to conventional practices, and so he says to the shepherd,

> [There] is another simple sin in you, to bring the ewes
> and the rams together and to offer to get your
> living by the copulation of cattle; to be bawd to a
> bell-wether, and to betray a she-lamb of a
> twelve-month to a crooked-pated, old, cuckoldly ram,
> out of all reasonable match. If thou beest not
> damned for this, the devil himself will have no
> shepherds.
>
> (*As You* III 2 74–80)

What is it that the fool is trying to do here? He is not really
questioning the practice of animal husbandry, nor is he opposed
to the principle of sexual attraction that runs through the whole
of creation. In *As You Like It*, when Touchstone brings his own
love to the multiple marriage feast in the Forest of Arden, he
exclaims that he too wants to be 'amongst the rest of the country
copulatives' (*As You* V 4 54). And in *All's Well That Ends Well*,
when the Countess asks the fool why he will marry, he replies
bluntly, 'My poor body, madam, requires it' (*All's Well* I 3 28). The
fool is in no sense a puritan about sexual desire. He wants people

to recognize what is within them and to name it. He also insists that they not unthinkingly accept convention.

The fool speaks truth to everyone but forces it on no one. No one is to be compelled to agree. And in the fool's world no one is to be eliminated for no one ultimately is a threat. As Feste says in *Twelfth Night*, 'that that is, is' (*Twelfth* IV 2 14). The fool in us essentially accepts the life that is in another. There may be much that we disagree with in another person but the fool in our depths knows that deeper still is the inherent value of the other. There is even a place for the enemy in the fool's world. In *Twelfth Night* when the Duke asks Feste how he is, the fool replies, 'the better for my foes, and the worse for my friends'. The Duke objects saying that surely it is 'the better for thy friends', but the fool explains,

> Marry, sir, they praise me – and make an ass of me.
> Now my foes tell me plainly, I am an ass; so that by
> my foes, sir, I profit in the knowledge of myself,
> and by my friends I am abused.
>
> (*Twelfth* V 1 9–19)

The Fool Within

The fool is calling us to be truly ourselves and points out the falseness of what we have become. He is not, however, over and against his hearers. Rather he invites them to discover the fool within themselves. In *All's Well That Ends Well*, when Parolles says that he has found the fool, the Clown replies, 'Did you find me in yourself, sir?' (*All's Well* II 4 32). The archetype of the fool is deep in the ground of our being. We may have lost contact with it or worked hard at covering it over, but it is there waiting to spring forth again.

In *King Lear* the fool calls the king a fool. When Lear asks him why, the fool replies, 'All thy other titles thou hast given away' (*Lear* I 4 147). Lear was born a fool, as were we all. Our other titles are superimposed and with time will fade. Lear has given his away prematurely and has forgotten his original self, including the fool in his depths. So out of touch is he with his own soul that he reacts to the description of the fool, who replies to Lear, 'Keep a schoolmaster that can teach thy fool to lie' (*Lear* I 4 175–6). Lear does not like what he hears so he wants to change it. He wants the fool to be taught otherwise. The suggestion is that we 'educate' the fool out of ourselves and out of one another. There is pressure on us to 'grow up' and to turn from the so-called foolishness of our childhood. Consequently some of our most natural ways of seeing become inhibited.

The fool in us is banished like the honest Cordelia in *King Lear*. She is rejected for speaking the truth. In the end, however, it is the simple and candid truthfulness of Cordelia that the king loves. When she is murdered he holds her in his arms and says, 'my poor fool is hanged' (*Lear* V 3 303). It is a picture of the way of the fool. The fool's way is costly. Often it is rejected by the world. And the rejection is not simply out there but in our own souls. To love the fool within ourselves is to be called repeatedly to let go. It is to stop grasping at what is passing.

The wisdom of the fool is something that is born with us in the womb. It is pure gift. We receive it rather than achieve it. In *As You Like It*, Touchstone, alluding to the Scriptures, says,

> . . . I do now remember a saying,
> 'The fool doth think he is wise, but the wise man
> knows himself to be a fool.'
>
> (*As You* V 1 28–30)

Wisdom's foolishness is not our possession. It is within us but comes from beyond us, and its flow is released in our lives not by trying to control it but by letting go to it. It is ours not on demand but in openness. In *Twelfth Night* the fool seeks wisdom in what is like a prayer of invocation,

> Wit, an't be thy will, put me into good fooling.
> Those wits that think they have thee do very oft
> prove fools; and I that am sure I lack thee may
> pass for a wise man.
>
> (*Twelfth* I 5 29–32)

The gift of foolishness appears in all sorts. It peeks out in the wit of the cobbler who describes himself as 'a mender of bad soles' (*Julius* I 1 14). It emerges in the gravedigger who claims to be the greatest of builders because the houses he builds last 'till Doomsday' (*Hamlet* V 1 59). It comes out in the simplicity of the gardener in *Richard II* who has observed from his little plot of earth what the king in all his sophistication and learning has never grasped politically, how to keep in check the various powers of the kingdom. 'O, what a pity is it', he says, that the king 'had not so trimmed and dressed his land as we this garden!' (*Richard II* III 4 55–7).

A type of wisdom even breaks through in the most ridiculous of characters, such as the foolish constable in *Much Ado About Nothing*, who says to the dastardly Borachio,

> O villain! Thou wilt be condemned into everlasting
> redemption for this.
>
> (*Much Ado* IV 2 54–5)

But as the penitent Borachio later says to the prince concerning his foolish captors, who caught him not because of their cleverness but because of their simpleness,

> ...what your wisdoms
> could not discover, these shallow fools have brought
> to light.
>
> (*Much Ado* V 1 221–3)

The so-called wise have missed what the foolish have stumbled upon. The fool in us can catch what the trained mind fails to see.

A glimpse of the fool's insight appears also in the half-witted weaver of *A Midsummer Night's Dream*. Nick Bottom wakes from the dream of midsummer night to say,

> The eye of man hath not heard, the ear of man hath not
> seen, man's hand is not able to taste, his tongue to
> conceive, nor his heart to report what my dream was!
> I will get Peter Quince to write a ballad of
> this dream. It shall be called 'Bottom's Dream',
> because it hath no bottom.
>
> (*Midsummer* IV 1 208–13)

Bottom in his foolishness ends up pointing to the depths of life rather than just its surface. Midsummer night has been a mystery of the seen and the unseen intermingled, of the unconscious at play beneath the conscious. Like the mystery of life it is a tale that has no 'bottom'. It cannot fully be told. Our attempts to describe it are only pointers. The fool in us knows the inadequacy of tight boundaries of definition. The mystery of our lives cannot be contained by understanding.

The fool breaks through in all sorts of characters. Sometimes, however, nothing of the fool's wisdom is to be seen. In *Twelfth Night* Sir Andrew Aguecheek is an entirely idiotic figure. He may have education and family lineage but there is no sign of insight in him, conscious or otherwise. He does, however, possess a type of recognition that wisdom is absent in his life. 'Methinks sometimes I have no more wit than a Christian', he says, 'but I am a great eater of beef, and I believe that does harm to my wit' (*Twelfth* I 3 80–2). Sir Andrew is consistently at the surface. Never does he dive more deeply. He is a picture of the fool and the contemplative in us entirely covered over.

The Distorted Contemplative

Within each of us is the true fool, even though we may be out of touch with that dimension of our being. So it is with the contemplative. All of the archetypes can be hidden. They also can be distorted and turned into shadow. The archetype of the contemplative is no exception. Our ability to perceive spiritually can be turned into an abuse of religious authority and power. The Cardinal in *King John* represents such an abuse. 'Be champion of our church,' he says to the King of France, 'or let the church, our mother, breathe her curse, a mother's curse, on her revolting son' (*John* III 1 255–7). It is the use of a tradition of spiritual insight to bully and to push into compliance. It denies a freedom of soul to its adherents.

There is the tendency also to turn spiritual insights into legalistic moralisms. What has its root in the liberty of truth becomes instead a caging in of life. In *The Merry Wives of Windsor* the priest, as well as teaching 'proverbs', is known for what are called his 'no-verbs' (*Merry* III 1 96). Our religious traditions become trapped in negative precepts and we end up missing the essential freedom that truth brings. Either that or we distort the expressions of collective spiritual insight to suit ourselves. In *As You Like It* the country vicar is called Sir Oliver Martext. We mar sacred truths when we tame them to serve our political and social prejudices. This is the complaint of one of the English lords in *2 King Henry IV* concerning the archbishop. He had been considered by the people 'deep ... within the books of God' and even 'th'imagined voice of God', but he turned 'the word to sword, and life to death', says the lord (*2 Henry IV* IV 2 4–22). The addition of one letter changes 'word' to 'sword'. So the slight twisting of spiritual insight perverts it from being life-giving to life-destroying. The archetypal energies of the contemplative in us are turned against our well-being instead of for our well-being.

One of the recurring shadows in the contemplative is the way in which we find it easier to translate our perceptions of truth into word than into action. In *King Lear* the fool says,

> I'll speak a prophecy ere I go:
> When priests are more in word than matter...
> Then shall the realm of Albion
> Come to great confusion.
>
> (*Lear* III 2 80–6)

As insights are released from our contemplative depths, if we do not apply them to our lives but leave them simply in the realm of perception, their truth will have no liberating power for us. If contemplative insights are not embodied in the 'matter' of our lives and world, we will continue to be slaves to 'great confusion'. Truth will be an opinion safely held rather than a passion that changes the way we live.

This is not to say that it is easy to practise what the contemplative preaches, nor is it to pretend that we should delay speaking truth until we are absolutely sure how to live it. A power to change our lives sometimes is released in the sheer act of uttering what we believe to be true. In *The Merchant of Venice* Portia says,

> ... It is a good divine that follows his own instructions;
> I can easier teach twenty what were good to be done,
> than to be one of the twenty to follow mine own teaching.
>
> (*Merchant* I 2 14–17)

It is easier to teach truth than to live it, but the discipline of trying to give expression to the contemplative in our depths can set in motion the desire to live from our depths. Equally the practice of living from our depths stirs within us further perceptions of what is true.

The most dangerous side of the contemplative is the power to manipulate the heart of another. We can use our knowledge of the soul not to set the other free but to have a type of power over the other. In *King Henry VIII* Norfolk says of Cardinal Wolsey,

> He dives into the King's soul, and there scatters
> Dangers, doubts, wringing of the conscience,
> Fears, and despairs...
>
> (*Henry VIII* II 2 25–7)

His insight provides him with the key of how to enter the heart of another, but once he has entered he works havoc rather than harmony. The king's queen, Katherine, names such abuse of spiritual authority. To Wolsey and his fellow cardinal she says, 'Ye have angels' faces, but heaven knows your hearts' (*Henry VIII* III 1 145). They have used the gifts of heaven to create bloody hell on earth.

The Birth of Contemplation

And yet the false Cardinal Wolsey repents. He turns from his shadow to the true contemplative, and in his repentant state reflects on his life journey which had been driven by a desperate desire to succeed,

> This is the state of man: today he puts forth
> The tender leaves of hopes, tomorrow blossoms,
> And bears his blushing honours thick upon him.
> The third day comes a frost, a killing frost,
> And, when he thinks, good easy man, full surely
> His greatness is a-ripening, nips his root,
> And then he falls, as I do. . . .
> Vain pomp and glory of this world, I hate ye.
> . . . O, how wretched
> Is that poor man that hangs on princes' favours!
>
> (*Henry VIII* III 2 352–67)

Wolsey now sees the imprisonment of living limitedly in outward terms, depending on the 'favours' of a prince or the prestige of outward success. 'Too much honour', he says, is a burden 'too heavy for a man that hopes for heaven' (*Henry VIII* III 2 385). Instead of liberating his soul it had chained him to his shadow.

Being stripped of outward honours, however, Wolsey comes to a new awareness,

> I know myself now; and I feel within me
> A peace above all earthly dignities,
> A still and quiet conscience.
>
> (*Henry VIII* III 2 378–80)

He has been set free by the disgrace of his fall to discover a deeper place of security within himself. To his friend Thomas Cromwell, he says,

> . . . fling away ambition:
> By that sin fell the angels. How can man then,
> The image of his Maker, hope to win by it?
> Love thyself last, cherish those hearts that hate thee;
> Corruption wins not more than honesty.
> . . . Be just, and fear not.
>
> (*Henry VIII* III 2 440–6)

Wolsey's words speak of the contemplative's freedom to live in relation to the law of our inner being. It is the law of loving others, even one's enemy. It is the law of doing what is true and just, and not fearing the consequences. It sets us free to be truly ourselves rather than striving to be someone other than ourselves. It is the freedom of living from the original pattern of our souls instead of from the falseness of what obscures our true depths. Wolsey has found in his downfall 'the blessedness of being little' (*Henry VIII* IV 2 66). Part of this 'blessedness of being little', as Wolsey's newfound freedom is described, is the realization of how little we need in terms of outward standing and recognition. It is combined also with the realization of how much we are inwardly. By birth we carry in our depths an infinite treasure. The contemplative within us sees this richness.

One of the great treasures that the contemplative is aware of is the place of inward sanctuary. It is a sacred space within us into which we may retreat for shelter and stillness. Entering the inner sanctuary is like passing a threshold that connects the world of time and the realm of the eternal. It is entering a silence that has always been. It is close to us, even within us, and yet it is not of our own making. We may have forgotten the sanctuary of stillness in the soul but the contemplative in us remembers it and knows the way to its portals.

One of the roles of the contemplative is to offer the gift of sanctuary to others, both physically and spiritually. The contemplative knows the places of sacred stillness and guards them in order to be able to share them. Here others may experience shelter from outward hostility and from inner tumult. In *The Comedy of Errors* the Abbess of Ephesus provides sanctuary for the pursued Antipholus of Syracuse thinking he is mad. Her intention is,

> With wholesome syrups, drugs and holy prayers,
> To make of him a formal man again.
>
> (*Comedy* V 1 104–5)

Rest and sanctuary are part of our healing. They are part of our becoming ourselves again. When those pursuing Antipholus demand his release, the Abbess replies firmly, 'Be quiet and depart: thou shalt not have him' (*Comedy* V 1 112). She is immovable. The contemplative in us knows the inviolable right of sanctuary. No person, no power has the right to deny the safe space, the confidentiality, the place of inner refuge that we can offer one another. 'The holy privilege of blessed sanctuary', as the priest in *Richard III* calls it (*Richard III* III 1 41), is essential to our inner well-being.

The contemplative within us knows about the importance of outward and inward sanctuary. It is not just about guarding that place for ourselves and for one another. It is also about guiding what happens in that place. In the shelter of sanctuary there is the safety of looking at what is within us. We can do that in our own souls. We can also enable others to do that. It is not that we know more about what is in the soul of others than they do. We can, however, be part of helping another see. As Hamlet says, it involves the holding up of a 'glass' or mirror to the soul of another to enable them to view their 'inmost part' (*Hamlet* III 4 21).

In Hamlet's case, the holding up of the mirror to another is complicated by the bitterness that is in him. It is not a safe sanctuary that he provides for his mother when he tries to force her into naming what is within her. He does, however, shift the queen towards facing some of her hiddenness. She says to him,

> O Hamlet, speak no more.
> Thou turnest mine eyes into my very soul,
> And there I see such black and grained spots
> As will not leave their tinct.
>
> (*Hamlet* III 4 89–92)

The effects of holding up the mirror to another can be painful. Hamlet knows that what his mother needs is not a 'flattering unction' for her soul, a soothing over of what is wounded in her. First of all she needs to confront the sickness in her soul, the shadow of her self. Any avoidance or skimming over of the wrongs that she is part of will only make things worse. As Hamlet says,

> It will but skin and film the ulcerous place
> Whilst rank corruption, mining all within,
> Infects unseen. Confess yourself to heaven.
> Repent what's past. Avoid what is to come;
> And do not spread the compost on the weeds
> To make them ranker.
>
> (*Hamlet* III 4 148–53)

Hamlet cannot repent for his mother, nor can his mother repent for him. The grace of repentance is not something that we can release in another person's soul, nor can anyone else do this for us. In that sense each of us is the ultimate carer for our own soul. When the false Macbeth, who has murdered his king and ordered the death of countless others throughout the realm, hopes that his wife, the accomplice in his crimes, can somehow be freed from the turbulence of her soul, he asks the doctor,

> Canst thou not minister to a mind diseased,
> Pluck from the memory a rooted sorrow,
> Raze out the written troubles of the brain,
> And with some sweet oblivious antidote
> Cleanse the stuffed bosom of that perilous stuff
> Which weighs upon the heart?
>
> (*Macbeth* V 3 39–44)

We can try, with the assistance of others, to numb our inner sensitivities to the wrongs we have done and attempt to deny them. In the end, however, they will eat away at the core of our well-being. Nothing can replace the need to consciously turn from the falseness of what we have become. As the doctor says to Macbeth,

> Therein the patient
> Must minister to himself.
>
> (*Macbeth* V 3 45–6)

In *Hamlet* the guilt-ridden Claudius comes close to repentance. He sees the inhumanity of what he has done, but he cannot bring himself to let go of the power and the privilege that he has won through his falseness. To his own soul he says,

O, my offence is rank. It smells to heaven.
It hath the primal eldest curse upon't,
A brother's murder. Pray can I not,
Though inclination be as sharp as will.
... But, O, what form of prayer
Can serve my turn? 'Forgive me my foul murder'?
That cannot be, since I am still possessed
Of those effects for which I did the murder,
My crown, mine own ambition and my Queen.
May one be pardon'd and retain th'offence?
... O, wretched state! O, bosom black as death!
O limed soul, that struggling to be free

Art more engaged! Help, angels! Make assay!
Bow, stubborn knees, and, heart with strings of steel,
Be soft as sinews of the newborn babe.
All may be well.

(*Hamlet* III 3 36–72)

But all is not well for Claudius because he refuses to turn around in his soul. He remains trapped in a hellish unrest within himself.

When we are being true to our contemplative depths, even when there is turbulence in our lives, we can be connected to a calm that is deeper than the disturbance. This gives rise to a stillness of perspective. In *Much Ado About Nothing*, amidst the hysteria at the marriage ceremony when the innocent bride is falsely accused of being faithless, the friar stands silent. He is searching beneath the surface for the truth that lies hidden from outward sight. When finally he speaks, he says,

Hear me a little;
For I have only silent been so long,
And given way unto this course of fortune
By noting of the lady. I have marked
A thousand blushing apparitions
To start into her face, a thousand innocent shames
In angel whiteness beat away those blushes;
And in her eye there hath appeared a fire,
To burn the errors that these Princes hold
Against her maiden truth. Call me a fool;
Trust not my reading nor my observations,
Which with experimental seal doth warrant
The tenor of my book; trust not my age,
My reverence, calling, nor divinity,
If this sweet lady lie not guiltless here
Under some biting error.

(*Much Ado* IV 1 153–68)

By being rooted more deeply than the storm the friar notes what is missed by others. As they are either carried away or outraged by the confusion, the contemplative sees from a place of stillness. And for the wronged bride in her pain he looks for the new thing that is trying to break through. 'On this travail look for greater birth', he says (*Much Ado* IV 1 211). The contemplative in us is forever alert to the beginnings that are on the other side of suffering. It is that part of our soul that knows that the current of life runs deeper than death.

The perspective of the contemplative is found not just in friars and abbesses. It is part of the human mystery. It is a dimension within every human being, although we may live at a tragic distance from it. We see it in someone like the Earl of Northumberland in *Richard II* who, in the midst of civil war, looks not away from the suffering of his country but through it to what is deeper still. Northumberland says,

> ... through the hollow eyes of death
> I spy life peering.
>
> (*Richard II* II 1 270–1)

In what can appear to be the most haunted places in our lives and world, the contemplative is looking for life's seed to be born in us in new ways. In the midst of suffering life is broken open. The contemplative searches what is being opened in us, and through the opening expects to see life 'peering'.

King Richard II is a character who is repeatedly broken. He is kinged and unkinged. At one moment he is all-powerful. At the next he is little more than a beggar, but he keeps missing the truth that is trying to appear to him through his struggles. At his lowest moment, however, in his final imprisonment he comes to the contemplative's perspective. 'Man', he says, 'with nothing shall be pleased till he be eased with being nothing' (*Richard II* V 5 40–1). When he has nothing left outwardly he discovers that within himself is everything. Only when he has lost the titles and the power which he had thought were everything are the depths and richness of his soul opened to him.

The challenge is to live from our contemplative depths even when we have not yet lost everything. Eventually we will lose everything. That is certain. But how do we live now in ways that free us from a dependence on the outward securities and successes of our lives? In *Romeo and Juliet*, the friar says to the distraught Romeo who has been banished from Verona and thinks he has lost everything that is most dear to him, 'birth, and heaven, and earth, all three, do meet in thee at once' (*Romeo* III 3 120–1). The friar sees that there is no moment in which 'birth and heaven and earth' do not meet. In every moment something new is waiting to be born. There is no situation in our lives in which the intercourse of heaven and earth does not conceive of new beginnings, even if that situation is of death or tragic loss. Life is forever surging up out of the unseen and the unknown into the visible and the conscious.

What is the relationship between the fool and the contemplative in us? The fool is pointing constantly to the edge where everything that we outwardly know and depend on is slipping away. There the contemplative looks for life and believes that as we let go we can be part of new conceptions. The fool says, 'from hour to hour we ripe, and ripe, and then from hour to hour we rot, and rot' (*As You* II 7 26–7). The contemplative says, 'on this travail look for greater birth' (*Much Ado* IV 1 211).

Appendix: Journalling Exercises

1: The King and the Queen

The archetype of the king and queen in us gives cohesion to our inner being. It represents that part of the soul that holds together the various energies that are within us. If it is not well, however, there can be chaos and misdirection in the entire realm of our life.

The following lines are from *3 King Henry VI*. The king has neglected his sovereignty and there is insurrection in the land. Henry wanders as a fugitive in his own kingdom, disguising his true identity. A shepherd asks him who he is, to which the king replies, 'More than I seem, and less than I was born to' (*3 Henry VI* III 1 56). When Henry finally admits to his kingship, the shepherd asks, 'But if thou be a king, where is thy crown?' (*3 Henry VI* III 1 61). The shepherd is looking for an outward sign of the king's authority.

Journalling Exercise

Enter the passage to develop the conversation between the king and the shepherd, using what Jung calls 'the active imagination' in which we employ fantasy to bring into consciousness an awareness of what is happening in our unconscious depths. Allow Henry to represent some aspect of your inner kingship/queenship that is weak. Let the shepherd's questions help you explore how to live in relation to your inner authority. Begin to journal your dialogue.

2: The Lover and the Friend

The archetypes of lover and friend represent that part of our soul that we can know only in relationship. The lover in us desires to give and receive from the centre of our being. It is that dimension of us that longs to fully trust another and to be stripped of the coverings that separate us. The friend similarly seeks mutuality in the giving and receiving of relationship. It is that part of us that feels at home in the company of the other.

The following passage is from *Julius Caesar*, in which Portia senses that something is not well within Brutus. She pleads with him to bare his soul:

> Is it expected I should know no secrets
> That appertain to you? Am I your self
> But, as it were, in sort or limitation,
> To keep with you at meals, comfort your bed,
> And talk to you sometimes? Dwell I but in the suburbs
> Of your good pleasure? If it be no more,
> Portia is Brutus' harlot, not his wife.

(*Julius* II 1 282–7)

Journalling Exercise

Enter the passage using the active imagination, allowing yourself to recall times in your life when you have not opened your soul to one who loves you. Recall the outward details of such moments and your inner feelings. Then, in relation to one of these times, let Portia's words address you and begin to journal your response. Allow yourself to speak from that part of you that longs to be fully open in relationship.

3: The Judge and the Warrior

The archetypes of judge and warrior relate to our capacity to know the truth. The judge in us discerns what is true and denounces what is false. The warrior in our depths is prepared to confront what is wrong and to fight for what is right. Both seek justice. The strength of the one is to see it and name it. The strength of the other is to battle for it and even to die for it.

The following lines are from *Measure for Measure* in which Isabella, the sister of the condemned Claudio, encourages the judge Angelo to consult his own heart. He has found Claudio guilty of fornication and has imposed the strictest of penalties, death. Isabella is not claiming that her brother is innocent. She is, however, pointing to the place of mercy in human relationship. 'Go to your bosom,' she says, 'knock there, and ask your heart what it doth know' (*Measure* II 2 136–7). Part of the truth that is within us is an empathy with those who have failed and a willingness to move through judgement to the possibility of transformation.

Journalling Exercise

Enter the passage using your imagination. Allow Isabella's words to address that part of you that is capable of seeing truth and confronting wrong. Recall a time in your life when you have opposed what is false but have allowed no place for mercy and new beginnings. Begin to journal your response to Isabella's words.

4: The Seer and the Mage

The archetypes of seer and mage relate to that part of us that is alive to the unknown and to the interweaving of the seen and the unseen. The mage within us uses wisdom to transform what is broken and torn in life.

The following passage is from *All's Well That Ends Well*. It is part of a dialogue between the King of France, who is suffering from what is thought to be an incurable disease, and the young Helena, a mage-like figure who has no status at court but who possesses a knowledge of the healing powers of plants.

King   We thank you, maiden,
But may not be so credulous of cure,
When our most learned doctors leave us, and
The congregated college have concluded
That labouring art can never ransom nature
From her inaidible estate. . . .

Helena   What I can do can do no hurt to try . . .
Dear sir, to my endeavours give consent.
Of heaven, not me, make an experiment . . .
But know I think, and think I know most sure,
My art is not past power, nor you past cure.

                (*All's Well* II 1 115ff.)

Journalling Exercise

Enter the passage imaginatively to develop the dialogue. Let the king represent the sovereign centre of your being, which in some way is unwell. Name your doubts about healing and allow Helena to be a hidden knowledge within you, given for your well-being. Begin to journal your dialogue.

5: The Fool and the Contemplative

The fool and the contemplative recognize that all things are passing. The fool knows and names that we are going to die. Everything is transitory, including the dignities and distinctions of life. The contemplative is alive also to what is not passing. It is that part of our soul that looks to the eternity out of which life comes forth and searches for the new beginnings that can emerge out of endings.

The following lines are from *Richard II*. In the face of civil war and chaos in the land, the Earl of Northumberland glimpses what is trying to be born amidst the agony of his nation. 'Through the hollow eyes of death,' he says, 'I spy life peering' (*Richard II* II 1 270–1). Pain breaks life open. The contemplative in us gazes at what is being torn apart by suffering, and through the opening expects to see life 'peering'. This is not to say that we know what will appear. Rather it is to let go of what we know in order to be open to what we do not yet know.

Journalling Exercise

Enter the passage imaginatively. Allow Northumberland to represent our contemplative depths. What are the sufferings within us and around us in our lives and world today? Let the contemplative in us name and face the pain of what is dying and listen to the expressions of trust in what is waiting to be born. Begin to journal what you hear within you.

Index